THE
DAY
APPROACHING

AMIR TSARFATI

HARVEST HOUSE PUBLISHERS
EUGENE, OREGON

Cover design by Faceout Studio

Cover Photo © Kayo, javarman, Jullius, KAMChokE / Shutterstock

The Day Approaching
Copyright © 2020 by Amir Tsarfati
Published by Harvest House Publishers
Eugene, Oregon 97408
www.harvesthousepublishers.com

ISBN 978-0-7369-8105-7 (pbk)
ISBN 978-0-7369-8106-4 (eBook)

Library of Congress Cataloging-in-Publication Data is on file at the Library of Congress, Washington, DC.

Printed in the United States of America

20 21 22 23 24 25 26 27 28 / LB-CD / 10 9 8 7 6 5 4 3 2 1

For my children Ariel, Maayan, Elad, and Eilon.
Because of you, my heart is proud and my life is full. I love you.

ACKNOWLEDGMENTS

First and foremost, I want to thank the Lord for His faithfulness throughout my life. Before I was even born, He loved me deeply and had a plan for my life. What a blessing it is to serve my Savior each and every day.

I want to thank my wife, Miriam, and my four children, whose love and support for me have never waned, even as the Lord has led me away from home so often. A husband and father could not be more blessed than I have been.

I want to thank my team at Behold Israel for their love, support, and dedication. H.T. and Tara, Mike and Sharon, Gale and Florene, Donalee and Jeff, Andy and Gail, Wayne and Cyndie, Joanne, Nick, Kayo, Tina, Jason, and Shane—the ministry wouldn't be what it is without your steadfast partnership.

Thank you to Barry Stagner and Rick Yohn for your wisdom and your rich insight into God's Word.

Thank you to Bob Hawkins Jr., Steve Miller, and the wonderful team at Harvest House.

Finally, thank you, Steve Yohn, for walking this journey with me.

CONTENTS

THE
DAY
APPROACHING

Let us hold fast the confession of our hope without wavering,
for He who promised is faithful. And let us consider one another
in order to stir up love and good works,
not forsaking the assembling of ourselves together,
as is the manner of some, but exhorting one another,
and so much the more as you see the Day approaching.

HEBREWS 10:23-25

CHAPTER 1

ANY DAY NOW

MANY MORNINGS I'LL WAKE UP, pour myself a cup of coffee, then take my Bible out to my back porch. As I settle into a cushioned chair, I'll take in the beautiful scene below me. Stretched out for miles is fertile land colored by whatever bountiful crop has been sown in it. Often there is a light breeze that the predatory birds take full advantage of as they hunt their scurrying prey. Taking in this beauty, my first thought is often, *Coffee is the greatest proof that there is a Creator God.* But my second thought is how unbelievable it is that conceivably in less than a decade or two that whole valley below me will be filling up with the armies of many nations. These armies will unite to march south to destroy the city of Jerusalem.

You see, that beautiful panorama below my backyard is the Jezreel Valley, also known as the Valley of Megiddo, also known as the Valley of Armageddon. If I see those armies gathering together, that will alert me to the following: First, I know that Israel has already endured a devastating attack—likely nuclear in nature. I know that a great world leader has arisen, uniting the nations of the world. I know that earthquakes and famines and other natural disasters have devastated the earth. I know that in Jerusalem a new temple has been built. And I know that the Mount of Olives is ready to feel the feet of the returning Savior, who will come as the King of kings and Lord of lords.

I also know that I will not be around to see any of this taking place. If those armies are down there, then I'm not up here—sipping on my coffee, enjoying the view. I'll already be in heaven. I'll be in the presence of my Savior, having been snatched up by Him seven years previously. And I'll be preparing to return with Him to this earth one more time. So, if you're planning on still being around at the end of the great tribulation, I'll leave the keys under the front mat for you—it should be quite a view.

God is working out His plan. There will soon be a day when the church is taken up to meet Jesus in the air. There will come a time when God disciplines the people of Israel in a way that ultimately leads to their repentance. And there will come a day when those who have rejected the free gift of God's salvation will suffer His wrath because of their sins.

The *what* of this coming day isn't the primary question of this book. I dealt with the rapture and the Antichrist in great detail in my previous book, *The Last Hour*. While we will deal with some of the events of the tribulation in *The Day Approaching*, our main focus here will be on the *when*.

Now, it's time for me to come 100 percent clean with you. I have no clue as to the day and time of Christ's return. But I'm in good company. No person knows the day and time. The angels don't know. Not even the Son of God Himself knows. Jesus said, "Of that day and hour no one knows, not even the angels of heaven, but My Father only" (Matthew 24:36). The Father has got the timing planned out to the minute, but He's keeping His cards close to His chest. What I can tell you is that as I look at the events unfolding in the world around us, I firmly believe that the day of Jesus' return is rapidly approaching.

I don't know about you, but I can't wait for that day when I see Jesus. I think about it. I imagine what it will be like. I study the Scriptures to learn all I can about it. This longing to see my Savior is not only in my heart, but also on my lips. I believe that we should proclaim our desire for Jesus to come. The apostle John wrote in the book of Revelation, "The Spirit and the bride say, 'Come!' And let him who hears say, 'Come!'" (22:17). John himself expressed his own desire when he said, "Even so, come, Lord Jesus!" (verse 20). Have you asked Jesus to come? Have you expressed to Him your excitement at seeing Him and your desire to be with Him forever? Have you ever taken a moment to close your eyes and picture what it will be like?

Imagine sitting around the dinner table with your family. You're about to take your first bite of your wife's wonderful spaghetti bolognese when you feel something happening—a tingling, a lightness—and suddenly, you are airborne. As you and your family shoot upward, you barely have time to see the look of wonder on their faces when another face catches your full attention. You recognize it immediately, even though you've never seen it before. It is the face of Jesus in all His glory and majesty. All the pains, fears, worries, and sorrows of the world are left behind in your recently departed dining room. Only joy, peace, and happiness await you as you enter into eternity.

This is the rapture. It is not just a story. It is not a feel-good religious fairy tale. It is an actual event that will take place in real time in the real world. I must admit that as I travel around the globe, I am amazed at how many people in the churches that I visit don't believe in the rapture. Others, more than not believing in it, are hostile to the whole idea. They don't even want to hear it mentioned.

I was speaking to a pastor friend of mine not long ago who told me that rather than looking forward to the advent of Christ's rule on earth, he believes we are now living in the kingdom of God. He says that all the events described in Revelation took place by AD 70. When Rome destroyed the temple and slaughtered thousands of Jews, the wrath of God was sated. No more need for judgment; no more need for hell. Our satisfied Lord will eventually save everyone. I was shocked to hear the extent of this pastor's deception.

We are living in a time of great anticipation surrounding the soon return of Christ, but it is also a time of great apostasy. Many antichrists exist in the world, both outside of the church and inside. As believers, we must know the truth of God's plan for mankind and how we fit into it. It is out of this knowledge that we find our mission and our hope.

GOD WANTS YOU TO KNOW HIS PLAN

The title of this chapter is "Any Day Now." If you have ever been on a tour with me, you will recognize this phrase immediately. I say these words probably 50 times a day to those who are casually finishing their cup of coffee or browsing for their next olive wood purchase while everyone else is waiting for them on the bus. It is often accompanied by an eye-roll or a wave of my watch. If these stragglers would have taken the time to look around, they would realize that they were the only members of the tour who weren't with the rest of the group.

If we take the time to look around us, we can't help but realize that there is a strong sense of Any Day Now in the world. It is so obvious to me, and I'm not the only one who feels it. In early 2017, the number of Google searches for "World War 3" hit its highest level ever. What precipitated this spike? The combination of President Donald Trump's escalation of activities in Syria and his dealings with North Korea.[1] Both of these situations have calmed since that moment of national panic, but there is still a sense that something significant is going on. Within us is a built-in curiosity about what is going to happen in the future, and a sense that the way the world is now must eventually come to an end.

Much of this curiosity stems from a fear of the unknown. Newspapers and 24-hour cable news channels are constantly bombarding readers and viewers with why they should be terrified if the US president does this or Iran does that or North Korea does something. Not long ago, a headline in *The Telegraph* read "World 'on the brink of thermo-nuclear war', as North Korea mulls test that could goad Trump."[2] Try getting a good night's sleep after reading that. People accuse Christians and the Bible of being doomsayers, but it's actually the media who are the doomsayers. In contrast, it's Christ and the Bible that give hope. It's Christ and the Bible that say, "Yes, eventually this world is going to blow apart. But let Me tell you how you can ensure yourself a flight out of here before it happens."

God wants you to know His plans—His plans for the world, for Israel, for the church, and for you. Are you interested in knowing the future? Then you need to go to the One who laid it out. He's already written what will happen; you just need to read it. Where should you start? All you need to know about what's coming was revealed through God's prophets.

These prophets were faithful yet tragic figures. The last thing anyone wanted to hear was God saying, "Guess what? I'm choosing you to be My prophet." The prophets were destined for a life of struggle, suffering, and pain. Yet nearly all raised their hands when God called. When the Lord asked, "Whom shall I send, and who will go for Us?," like Isaiah, they stepped up and said, "Here am I! Send me" (Isaiah 6:8).

These days, everybody wants to be a prophet. I guess it's because there is profit in being a prophet. I am not a prophet. I come from a nonprofit organization. Today's prophets teach their own opinions and call them words from the Lord. But man's opinion doesn't come close to meeting the biblical standard for prophecy. "No prophecy of Scripture is of any private interpretation, for prophecy never came by the will of man, but holy men of God spoke as they were moved by the Holy Spirit" (2 Peter 1:20-21). When Jeremiah and Isaiah and Hosea and Malachi and all the other prophets spoke prophetically, they were not speaking their own thoughts and viewpoints. Prophecy originates in the mind of God, and then is spoken through the mouths of His chosen messengers.

God's prophetic message—His plan for this world—has been revealed to us in the Bible. From Genesis to Revelation, the Lord lays out His blueprint for eternity step by step and piece by piece. Despite the fact He has given us 66 books of revelation, there are many who look only to the New Testament for their eternal guidance. They assume that the Old Testament was just fine for its time, but then Jesus came along and brought the New. The Old was great for the Jews, but we're the church. Who wants the Old when you can have the New and improved?

So much of what God wants us to know about the future is found in the distant past—before the church and the New Testament. If we limit ourselves to Matthew 24–25 and the book of Revelation, we will get only part of the story. In Hebrews we read that "God, who at various times and in various ways spoke in time past to the fathers by the prophets, has in these last days spoken to us by His Son" (1:1-2). The God who spoke His truth through Jesus and the New Testament writers is the same God who pulled back the curtain on the end times through the Old Testament prophets.

When we read the words of Malachi or Zechariah or Hosea, we

know they are from the mouth of the Lord. The prophet was just a spokesperson. He likely understood very little of what he saw and said. In fact, in many cases, today we understand much more than the prophets ever did about what God is going to do as He brings salvation to the church, discipline to the Jews, and wrath upon the earth. And so much of what we see in the prophets and the New Testament seems to indicate that this great Day of the Lord is coming closer and closer.

THE TIMES ARE MOVING FORWARD

History is moving forward, and the events that are rapidly approaching can be separated into two categories: those we can do something about, and those we can't. Most future happenings fall into the latter category. When the angel Gabriel came to the prophet Daniel, he told him what was definitely going to happen. He said, "Seventy weeks are determined for your people and for your holy city" (Daniel 9:24). The events that Gabriel spoke of *will* take place—they've been determined. You can try to stop the works of God, but you won't get very far. Imagine a speeding train hurtling in your direction. It doesn't matter how earnestly you desire to stop it, that's not going to happen. You can brace your feet. You can grit your teeth. You can scream at the train with all your might, "Thou shalt not pass!" Still, within moments, the train will run right over you and you'll be flattened like a pita.

If the world's future is so much out of our control, does that mean we are utterly doomed? Is there anything we can do to give ourselves hope in God's grand plan? Most certainly. We can choose to follow Christ, giving ourselves to Him as our Lord and Savior. If we do that, then we are assured that when He returns for His church, we will be taken to Him.

However, if we choose to reject Him—or even if we simply

ignore the choice, which is the same as turning our backs on Him—we will be left to experience the terrors of judgment. What a simple choice! Either we choose life eternal or we choose death. We will choose to escape the wrath of God, or we will choose to experience the tribulation and suffer for all eternity apart from our Creator. There is no other decision that we can make in our life that presents such a stark contrast. Praise the Lord that He has given us the opportunity to choose Him! But the day of choosing is now.

Why must it be now? Because the time left for making a choice may soon come to an end. As we keep our eyes on the news, it seems more and more as if the final days are nearly at hand. One key sign of the day approaching will take place in Syria. Isaiah prophesied that Damascus will one day be utterly annihilated: "Behold, Damascus will cease from being a city, and it will be a ruinous heap" (17:1). Up until recently, most people in the world had never even heard about Damascus. Those who did knew it as the "City of Jasmine," with a wonderful historical and modern culture. But now, as the center of the Syrian conflict, the city is on the front page of the newspapers almost daily. As hostilities not only continue but increase, it is not hard to envision the eventual leveling of that ancient city.

The times are moving forward. The Lord is shifting all the players into position and is setting up the playing field. Just one example of God's logistical work that would have been unheard of a mere decade ago relates to plans for a project under the Mediterranean Sea. This will be the longest underwater pipeline in the world, from Israel to Italy. This pipeline will carry natural gas from Israel's recently found gas fields to the European Union. Sounds wonderful, doesn't it? It does if you're not from Russia. What Putin and his cronies see is an upstart nation stealing their customers. Russia, whose economy is already shaky, can't afford to lose the European market, and they won't just sit by and watch their largest customer get taken away.

There are three truths that become evident as we observe current events. First, the events prophesied in the Word of God are taking shape all around us. The new ideas and plans of today's world leaders were known and talked about by God 2,800 years ago. There is no move that can be made that will take God off-guard. There is no strategy that can be implemented that He has not considered. King Solomon writes, "The king's heart is in the hand of the Lord, like the rivers of water; He turns it wherever He wishes" (Proverbs 21:1). When presidents and kings and prime ministers believe they are exercising their own great power and authority, they are actually following God's lead.

Second, there is a smoke screen of deception surrounding world events that is confusing many people. They are buying into the lies proclaimed by the media and politicians. An example of this fake news has to do with the chemical attacks by Syrian President Bashar al-Assad upon his people. One group of people say, "Of course he did it. That's the kind of person he is." While others say, "How can you say such a thing? He would never do that to his people."

Even Christians get caught up in this kind of duplicity and fight amongst each other. Why? Is it so surprising that Syria would gas its own people? I'll let you in on a little secret if you promise to keep it just between us: I know the name of the Syrian pilot who dropped chemical bombs on his people. I know the name of his aircraft. The Israeli government knows his address and phone number. We know where he took off from, when he did it, and we have a video of him dropping the bombs. Yet Christians still argue over whether these kinds of things have happened. Why do we let Satan divide us over politics and opinions?

Still, in the midst of all the deception and division, we see tremendous acts of God's people showing His love. On Palm Sunday of 2017, there was a horrific attack in Egypt. ISIS targeted two

Coptic churches, and the bomb blasts killed 47 and injured at least 109.[3] So many lives taken, so many bodies maimed. Yet how did the leaders of the Coptic church respond? Believe it or not, they thanked ISIS. You may wonder how that is possible after such an atrocity. First, they thanked the terrorists because they had sent 47 people into the arms of Jesus. In the moment of that blast, those who were killed saw their Savior face to face. Second, since that attack, their churches have been absolutely packed. All those who were lazy about coming to worship are now running to church.

As if thanking their enemies was not enough, the leaders of the Coptic church followed up by telling their ISIS attackers, "We love you." They told the extremists that they understood they are caught up in a lie and don't know the truth. Finally, the church leaders went one step further. They said, "And we commit to praying for you."[4] This put Jesus' words from the Sermon on the Mount into flesh: "Love your enemies, bless those who curse you, do good to those who hate you, and pray for those who spitefully use you and persecute you, that you may be sons of your Father in heaven" (Matthew 5:44-45). These brothers and sisters of the Coptic church showed themselves to be sons and daughters of their Father in heaven and ambassadors of the love of their Savior.

For those of us who are Christians, death has truly lost its sting. Christ in us allows us to love our enemies and pray for those who would do us harm. This is because we can see the bigger picture. We have not become lost in the smoke screen of deception. We know that for us, "to live is Christ, and to die is gain" (Philippians 1:21). No longer should we be afraid of death. When our time comes, we can go happily into that dark night knowing that the light of eternal life awaits us.

The third truth we learn from observing current events is that God is revealing Himself to people all around the world. There are changes taking place in people's hearts and the gospel is finding its way into places never before reached. This is the direct hand of God at work. I receive hundreds of emails and messages every day from every corner of the globe—Malaysia, the Philippines, Japan, North America, Australia, South America, Israel, Europe. What so many of these people are writing is, "Amir, I'm having visions," or "Amir, I keep having these dreams." The prophet Joel wrote:

> God is moving.
> He is speaking.
> He is coming soon.

> It shall come to pass afterward
> that I will pour out My Spirit on all flesh;
> your sons and your daughters shall prophesy,
> your old men shall dream dreams,
> Your young men shall see visions.
> And also on My menservants and on My maidservants
> I will pour out My Spirit in those days (Joel 2:28-29).

These people who write to me say that God has spoken to them in a clear way, saying, "I am coming soon." People in China and Mexico and New Zealand are all hearing the same message independently from one another. God is moving. He is speaking. He is coming soon.

As we read the newspapers and watch the cable channels, a contrast becomes evident. On the one hand, everything seems to be falling apart. The talking heads will tell you nightly that we're all doomed and a nuclear holocaust is right around the corner. On the other hand, when we look through the lens of Scripture, everything is falling into place. The newspaper writers can't see it. They are trying to make sense of what's going on without having the capacity to understand. It's like small children trying to explain quantum physics—they simply don't have the capacity to do that. But when we look at world events through the lens of the Bible, we find the key to unlocking the truth.

"But wait," you may say, "the news and the Bible are two different things. The news is about now. The Bible is history and was written thousands of years ago." True, the Bible is history. But the Bible is also His story. It is the story of God's plan for this earth from the very beginning to the very end. In the pages of Scripture, you will find what was, what is, and what is yet to come. In fact, what you see happening in many of the nations today is right out of the Bible.

"Wait, Amir, are you going to tell me that Russia is in the Bible?" Yes! "Egypt and Ethiopia are in the Bible?" Yes and yes! "Iran and Turkey and Sudan?" Yes, yes, and yes! Much of what you see around you with the growing world powers and their alliances is straight out of the pages of biblical prophecy.

Ezekiel 38 tells us of the evil intentions of Russia when it describes how Ros will be led down to Israel as if a hook were put into its jaw. Ros will come down not for the purpose of peace, but plunder. Today, the Russians are the number one player in the Syrian civil war, and they don't even try to hide the fact that they are there primarily for the gas and oil. Russia's only warm-water seaport giving access to the Mediterranean and the Middle East is in Syria. That's why Russia backs the government of Bashar al-Assad.

Who does Ezekiel say will be aligned with Ros? None other than Persia, which is modern-day Iran. The Iranians' goal is to be poised on Syria's border with Israel so that when the attack does come, they will be ready to pour into the Jewish state. Also in this Russian alliance are Sudan and Libya. The Russians have long had an interest in the oil fields of Libya and are looking for opportunities to put their nose under the Libyan tents. Oil, gas, Russia—it is no surprise to find them linked together again.

Standing with Israel against these enemies are Jordan and,

through more recent and unofficial alliances, Saudi Arabia and Egypt. Surprisingly to many, the Saudis have signed a secret deal with Israel, saying, "If you want to attack Iran, feel free to use our airspace."[5] The Saudis did add a caveat promising that if Israel admitted to this alliance, they would deny it and condemn Israel in the UN. Is this secret alliance with Saudi Arabia spoken of in the Bible? No. But long before that region was called Saudi Arabia, it was called Sheba and Dedan. "Sheba, Dedan, the merchants of Tarshish, and all their young lions will say to you, 'Have you come to take plunder? Have you gathered your army to take booty, to carry away silver and gold, to take away livestock and goods, to take great plunder?'" (Ezekiel 38:13). Saudi Arabia will not join in the attack against Israel because they are allies. But neither will Saudi Arabia try to stop it. They will stand by ready to collect the spoils of what they assume will be a devastated nation.

And who is standing there next to the Saudis ready to scavenge? The merchants of Tarshish and all their young lions—Europe (the home of the city of Tarshish) and America (the ferocious young nation that was birthed out of Europe). Some 2,000, 3,000, even 4,000 years ago, God knew the identity of the players on today's political stage. Using the names of the countries in those times, He explained exactly what His future plans are.

THE SIGNS OF THE TIMES

One day in the midst of all the crazy busyness of His ministry, Jesus took a break. He left the temple, went through a gate in the walls of Jerusalem, and walked up the Mount of Olives. There He sat by Himself and took in the view of the Holy City. Whether He was thinking or praying or just enjoying the silence, we don't know. What we do know is that His private moment didn't last long. The disciples had been troubled by something that Jesus had just said to them at the temple. They had been oohing and aahing over the beauty of the temple, but rather than admiring the magnificent structure along with them, the Lord had said, "Do you not see all these things? Assuredly, I say to you, not one stone shall be left here upon another, that shall not be thrown down" (Matthew 24:2).

Troubled, the disciples approached Him for some answers. "Tell us, when will these things be? And what will be the sign of Your coming, and of the end of the age?" (verse 3).

Rather than rebuff them or plead His need for a little "Me" time, Jesus gave them an amazing answer. He told them that people would come seeking to deceive them and claim that Christ has returned. Wars and rumors of wars will have people shaking in their sandals, but the disciples were not to be afraid. "For nation will rise against nation, and kingdom against kingdom. And there will be famines, pestilences, and earthquakes in various places. All these are the beginning of sorrows" (verses 7-8). The world is going to get violent and dangerous, Jesus said, but that's just the beginning.

Look around the world today. Did Jesus just describe our time? Earthquake activity continues to increase. In just the last 6 years we have seen major volcanic eruptions from Mount Etna (Italy), Mount Sinabung (Indonesia), Mount Kelud (Indonesia), Mount Ontake (Japan), and Mount Calbuco (Chile). In 2018, Volcán de Fuego blew in Guatemala, killing 190 people. Later that same year, the infamous Anak Krakatoa in Indonesia erupted, which caused a tsunami that killed nearly 450 people and injured more than 14,000 more.[6] Famine continues to spread too. The UN has declared famine conditions in South Sudan, Yemen, Nigeria, and Somalia.[7] This desperate lack of food is not due to weather conditions but is mostly the result of rampant government corruption. All of what Jesus described exists today in our world, and in ever-increasing intensity.

How do you feel when you watch the news? Do you get nervous?

Do you stay awake at night worrying? Let me tell you, there is no reason to stay awake. I live in a very safe country. However, I also live in a nation that is hated by most of the people who surround us. Many times I've had my day interrupted by an app on my phone that alerts me when rockets are fired from Gaza or the West Bank into Israel. Imagine if rockets were regularly fired across your borders into your country. Despite that, I sleep like a baby every night. My peace comes from the fact that even if a rocket happened to break through our Iron Dome missile defense and land on the roof of my house, my family and I would wake up in the presence of our Savior. And in that coming time when Russia finally decides to take what belongs to Israel, it can drop all the bombs it wants on my house. My family and I won't be there. We'll be testing out our new bodies with the rest of the raptured church.

The news is bleak and the world is on a downward slide. The Bible says that when you begin to see these things take place, don't let your head droop down in sorrow. Instead, look up—your redemption is drawing near. Does that excite you? It should. Jesus is returning for His church, and we could meet Him in the clouds any day now.

CHAPTER 2

THE FIG TREE AND THE FINAL GENERATION

NOT LONG AGO, I WAS HAVING DINNER in the home of a friend in America. After the meal, all the dishes were taken into the kitchen and the familiar sounds of the post-dinner cleanup were heard. As my friend and I retired to his living room, the growl of the garbage disposal carried from the kitchen. "A week ago, you wouldn't have heard that sound," he said. Intrigued, I asked him to elaborate.

A week earlier, his disposal had jammed. This wasn't the first time, so he began his usual clear-the-disposal routine. First, he slid his hand through the sink drain to make sure nothing was blocking it. There wasn't. Second, he checked underneath the sink to make sure it was still plugged in. It was. Third, he retrieved a broom and used the broom handle to try to budge the blades. They were budgeless. The situation was beginning to seem hopeless as he stood there with his stinky hand holding a scarred broom. Defeated, he called a plumber.

Three hours later, the plumber arrived. Before he even looked at the disposal unit, he asked, "Did you press the reset button?"

"The what?"

The plumber opened the cabinet and kneeled down, thankfully pulling up the back of his pants before he did so. He reached his hand around to the back of the unit, then stood up, turned on the water, and flipped the disposal switch. The machine whirred to life. That was how my friend learned that his garbage disposal had a reset button. It had only cost him three hours, a $120 charge, and all his male dignity.

For us to truly understand what the Lord is saying to us in the Gospels and the rest of the Bible, we need to press our own reset button. We bring so many traditions and presuppositions into our biblical interpretations that it is often difficult to just read the Bible as it is written. So before you read further, take your finger, rest it against the side of your head, and press firmly. There! You've just reset your brain. Now you can read on.

It's very important to understand that when Jesus came 2,000 years ago, He did so as a Jew to the Jewish people. You would be surprised how many people aren't aware of this fact. I take people on tours all around Israel, and they see churches built up on many of the historical sites. Sometimes they pull me aside and want to know which one Jesus attended. "Amir, was Jesus Catholic, Orthodox, or Anglican?" "None of the above," I answer, "because Jesus was one hundred percent a Jew."

When Jesus taught His Jewish disciples, much of the time He did so in Jerusalem—the capital of Israel. Jerusalem was the capital then, and it is the capital now, no matter what the rest of the world wants to say. In fact, it has been the capital of Israel ever since David made it so 3,000 years ago. So Jesus, as a Jew, taught Jews Jewish things. And the subjects the disciples asked about were also completely Jewish in nature—issues related to the temple, the Messiah, and the last days. The Gentiles weren't into that kind of stuff. What did they care about believing in one God, a strange temple that had no statue of a deity in it, sitting around and doing nothing one specific day of the week, and strange beliefs about the last days? But these were the very subjects the Jewish disciples wanted to learn about.

THE PARABLE OF THE FIG TREE

In Matthew 24 and Luke 21, we read about Jesus taking His disciples up to the Mount of Olives, which overlooked the temple. It was a powerful sight, and the disciples got to thinking. They asked Jesus some questions of genuine importance, which He welcomed. Gathering them around, He took time to explain the events of that era and of the future.

Isn't it awesome how we can come to God searching for truth and He will never turn us away? James tells us that if a person is wrestling with an issue, "let him ask of God, who gives to all liberally and without reproach, and it will be given to him" (James 1:5). Whether we are facing a major life decision or we need help trying to figure out a difficult biblical passage, the Holy Spirit is there to guide us and reveal His truth to us.

Jesus answered the disciples' questions in a passage that has come to be known as the Olivet Discourse because it was given on the Mount of Olives. Found in Matthew 24, it can be divided into two parts: the future of Israel (Matthew 24:4-31), and the future of the church (Matthew 24:32-51). In the first portion, Jesus speaks to the disciples as Jews. In the second, He talks to them as members of the soon-to-be church.

Wedged in between those two significant passages is a short

pause of sorts—a four-verse tangent that is both significant and remarkable. Here, Jesus tells a parable about a fig tree:

> Now learn this parable from the fig tree: When its branch has already become tender and puts forth leaves, you know that summer is near. So you also, when you see all these things, know that it is near—at the doors! Assuredly, I say to you, this generation will by no means pass away till all these things take place. Heaven and earth will pass away, but My words will by no means pass away (Matthew 24:32-35).

The first important point to recognize is that Jesus says this is a parable. This is not a horticulture lesson. This is not a farmer's almanac. Jesus is telling a story about something that represents something else.

He also says that when the fig tree starts sprouting, "you know" that it is almost summer. Those are important words. You are not just hoping for the summer or longing for the summer. There is no doubt that a sprouting tree means that spring is about to move off the scene and be replaced by warmer weather. Once more, Jesus says that when you "see" these signs, you will know that the time is near. You will not simply hear about the sprouting fig tree or think about it or maybe dream about it. You, with your own two eyes, will recognize these signs and know their implications.

Again, these verses serve as a transition between Jesus' message to the Jews and His message to the church. It is here that Jesus is shifting His conversation with the disciples, speaking to them first as the former and then as the latter. They are not just Jews, they are also part of the family of God.

When the church began, it was primarily Jewish. It took until Acts 15 and the Council at Jerusalem for the Jewish believers to figure out what to do with these Gentiles who had begun pouring in, eating their bacon and lobster rolls. Those of us who are Jewish believers must live in both worlds. Ethnically, I am Jewish, but Israel is not where my true citizenship belongs. As soon as I became a believer, my citizenship shifted—I received a new passport. "For our citizenship is in heaven, from which we also eagerly wait for the Savior, the Lord Jesus Christ, who will transform our lowly body that it may be conformed to His glorious body, according to the working by which He is able even to subdue all things to Himself" (Philippians 3:20-21).

Yes, we as Christians have an earthly citizenship, but our first loyalty is to the kingdom of God. We are just sojourners on this earth. When our time on earth is over, we are going to our true home.

HOW LONG IS A GENERATION?

What is the purpose of the fig tree parable? It is to identify the generation that will not pass away before the world, as we know it, draws to a conclusion. That's pretty exciting when you stop to think about it. Imagine being part of that final generation that sees God's end game playing out. But what does it mean to be part of this generation that will not pass away? Before we can answer that question, we have an even more basic one to deal with: What is a generation? This may seem simple, but many have wrestled with the definition of this crucial word over the ages.

Some say that a generation equals the longevity of mankind. In other words, it is one human life-span long. While preaching in Pisidian Antioch, Paul equated the word "generation" with the length of David's life. He said, "David, after he had served his own generation by the will of God, fell asleep, was buried with his fathers, and saw corruption" (Acts 13:36). In this biblical context, a generation begins at conception and ends at death.

And yes, life does begin at conception. David the psalmist wrote, "Your eyes saw my substance, being yet unformed. And in Your book they all were written, the days fashioned for me, when as yet there were none of them" (Psalm 139:16). God's plan for every person begins even before they are formed in the womb. I know a man who went through fertilization treatments with his wife. Just prior to the procedure in which the fertilized eggs were placed into her womb, this soon-to-be father was brought to a microscope. There, he saw his daughter 6 days after conception. She was merely a little mass of cells. Now she's 18 years old and preparing for college. What he saw through that microscope was no less human—no less alive—than what he will soon see walk onto a stage to receive her high school diploma.

Biblically, there is no pro-life versus pro-choice debate. The opposite of pro-life is pro-death. That is what our world's abortion culture promotes. Moses, just before he died, called the people of Israel together and offered them a choice. "I call heaven and earth as witnesses today against you, that I have set before you life and death, blessing and cursing; therefore choose life, that both you and your descendants may live" (Deuteronomy 30:19). With God, the choice is always life.

According to the theory that a generation refers to the length of a person's life, a generation is equal to the average life span of a group of people living at about the same time. Before the biblical flood, the average life span of mankind was around 900 years. Can you imagine that? You meet someone on the street and ask him how old he is. "Oh, six hundred or so. It's hard to remember exactly after so long."

"Six hundred? I can't even remember my six hundreds, they were so long ago," you reply. "When we lit my last birthday cake, my house burned down."

I don't know about you, but I don't want to live that long in this body. I haven't even reached half a century in age, and I'm already tired of it. I'm ready for the incorruptible upgrade I'm going to get when Jesus returns.

A second option for determining the length of a generation is by using what is called a "wilderness generation." This uses the length of the Hebrew wanderings in the wilderness as the definition. When the Israelites refused to trust God and enter the Promised Land, He swore an oath of punishment against them:

> "Surely none of the men who came up from Egypt, from twenty years old and above, shall see the land of which I swore to Abraham, Isaac, and Jacob, because they have not wholly followed Me, except Caleb the son of Jephunneh, the Kenizzite, and Joshua the son of Nun, for they have wholly followed the LORD." So the LORD's anger was aroused against Israel, and He made them wander in the wilderness forty years, until all the generation that had done evil in the sight of the LORD was gone (Numbers 32:11-13).

A 40-year period of time was required for the disobedient generation of Moses' day to die off in the wilderness.

However, those who hold to the 40-year generation concept do not take into account the total age of those who had sinned against the Lord. The curse was given against those who had reached 20 years of age and older. After the 40-year judgment period was completed, there were no men left beyond 60 years of age except Joshua and Caleb. So that would have to be the number used to determine the length of a generation—20 plus 40. But 20 was just the minimum. There could have been people who lived much longer. If someone was 50 when the judgment was pronounced, he or she could have lived all the way to age 90 before dying in the wilderness. Then there were also the outliers—Aaron died at age 123, Moses reached 120, Joshua was 110 when he died, and Caleb was somewhere past 85.

I believe the answer to the generational question lies in the Psalms. In Psalm 90 we find a special poem. It is the oldest psalm in the Bible, and it is the only one written by Moses. Here, this great prophet wrote, "All our days have passed away in Your wrath; we finish our years like a sigh. The days of our lives are seventy years; and if by reason of strength they are eighty years, yet their boast is only labor and sorrow; for it is soon cut off, and we fly away" (Psalm 90:9-10).

If ever there was doubt that Moses was a Jew, all one needs to do is to read this depressing passage. The two verses are one long groan. What's noteworthy here is the life span Moses lays out. Our days are 70 years, but if you're working out, watching your fat intake, and remembering your vitamins, then maybe you'll make it to 80. That is the length of a life.

This is similar to the life span theory we looked at earlier—Moses lays out a generation as being from birth to death. The early mega-year people who lived before the flood were outliers. The next time you are in church, look around, and you will likely see a generation of people. You will see some newborns and you will see some of the dear saints in their nineties. This is the length of a generation—somewhere between 70-100 years.

THE THREE PLANTS OF ISRAEL

Now that we've determined the length of a generation, we need to identify who this generation is that Jesus speaks of. There are some who suggest He was talking about the people who were alive during the time He spoke the parable. Others say that the generation refers to the people of Israel in their entirety. But neither one of those options works. The reason they don't is because of the identity of the tree. The fig tree that Jesus speaks of is Israel itself. Based on that fact, Jesus' generation could hardly say that the Israel of the first century was tender and putting forth leaves. Rather, they were under oppressive Roman rule. In fact, just four decades after Jesus told this parable, the Romans would wreak havoc upon Jerusalem and destroy the temple. The Jewish people themselves are also disqualified from being the generation. Remember, they are the fig tree. You can't both watch for the sign and be the sign.

"But, Amir," you say, "where does Jesus say that Israel is the fig tree?" He doesn't, but the prophets do. In the Bible, the nation of Israel is likened to three different plants—the vine, the olive tree, and the fig tree. The vine is the symbol of Israel's spiritual privileges. "You have brought a vine out of Egypt; you have cast out the nations, and planted it" (Psalm 80:8). Jesus, as a Jew, is not only part of the vine, but is Himself the true Vine. He says, "I am the vine, you are the branches. He who abides in Me, and I in him, bears much fruit; for without Me you can do nothing" (John 15:5). Jesus is the vine, and we who are in the church are the branches, which bear spiritual fruit. Thus, both Israel and the church have their identity closely connected to the vine.

The same is true with the olive tree: "I will be like the dew to Israel; he shall grow like the lily, and lengthen his roots like Lebanon. His branches shall spread; his beauty shall be like an olive tree, and his fragrance like Lebanon" (Hosea 14:5-6). This gnarled tree is a symbol of Israel's religious privileges. What a blessing it is for the church to be allowed to be grafted into the tree, sharing in the privileges given to Israel. "And if some of the branches were broken off, and you, being a wild olive tree, were grafted in among them, and with them became a partaker of the root and fatness of the olive tree, do not boast against the branches. But if you do boast, remember that you do not support the root, but the root supports you" (Romans 11:17-18).

Praise the Lord, those of you who are in the church are now partakers of the root and fatness of the olive tree. Abraham, the father of the Jews, is now your father also. The Old Testament is now your book too. The church is fully assimilated into all the traditions and writings of Jewish history. But Paul warned, "Don't let this go to your head, church folk. Remember, you were grafted into them, not the other way around."

It is a different story when we come to the fig tree. "I found Israel like grapes in the wilderness; I saw your fathers as the firstfruits on the fig tree in its first season" (Hosea 9:10). This tree is a symbol of Israel's national privileges, and, as such, the church has no part of it. There is no assimilating—no grafting in—because it is in the fig tree that we find the Jews' ownership over the land, their ownership over Jerusalem, and their return to the homeland. The church cannot *be* the fig tree; it can only *see* the fig tree.

There are so many in the church who want to be the fig tree—they want to be Jews. In one sense, I can understand that. Recently, a friend emailed me and said that his parents had taken a DNA test. When the results came back, his mother discovered that her father, whom she had never known, was fully Jewish. This made my friend one-quarter Jew. I responded, "Exciting discovery—that explains why you're so brilliant!" However, if you are one of those who wishes you were Jewish, let me suggest you point your aspirations in a different direction. All you need to do is look at a little history to realize that being a Jew isn't always all it's cracked up to be.

Besides, as a Gentile, you cannot be part of the fig tree or grafted into it. No matter how much you wish to be a Jew, you cannot be one. It is not in your genes. You may wish you were 6'4" and an NFL linebacker, but if both your parents were 5'3" it's not going to happen. Is that right or wrong? No, it just is. You can be part of the olive tree and the vine because they have to do with spiritual and religious privileges. But the fig tree is all about national privileges, and those privileges belong to the people of the Jewish nation.

If, as a Gentile, your desire is to be a Jew, then you are missing out on your vital role in God's plan. Paul says in Romans 11 that you are to help provoke the Jews to jealousy. So why are you being provoked to jealousy by them and wanting to be Jewish? Instead, the church should be showing Israel just how wonderful it is to have a close, personal relationship with God—the relationship that the Lord originally intended to have with them. What is the ultimate goal of stirring up that jealousy? According to Paul, it is to "save some of them. For if their being cast away is the reconciling of the world, what will their acceptance be but life from the dead?" (Romans 11:14-15).

If you love the Jewish people, then what better way is there to show it than by embracing your close church-relationship with the Savior of the world, and thereby fulfilling your part in God's plan to bring salvation to the Jews?

THE BRANCH PUTS FORTH LEAVES

Back to the fig tree—since this is a parable, we understand that Jesus is not really talking about the fig tree. Instead, He is referring to the nation represented by the fig tree. He says, "Sure, they will be scattered and near death. They will be hated and surrounded by their enemies. The land itself will become desolate and barren. But there will come a generation that will see the resurrection of this nation represented by the fig tree."

Historically, this is exactly what happened to Israel. The desolation of the Promised Land began with the Roman siege of Jerusalem and the destruction of the temple in AD 70. It was solidified when Julius Severus, under orders from the Emperor Hadrian, put down the Bar Kokhba revolt in AD 135. Jerusalem was renamed Aelia Capitolina, and Judea became Syria Palestina. These events began the rapid decline of the land that was once marveled over by foreign dignitaries during the time of King David and King Solomon.

At the beginning of the twentieth century, Judea was still a dry wasteland, occasionally relieved by marshy and malarial swamp-lands. Yet God promised that would change. All it took for the land to be restored was God's own words.

> You, O mountains of Israel, you shall shoot forth your branches and yield your fruit to My people Israel, for they are about to come. For indeed I am for you, and I will turn to you, and you shall be tilled and sown. I will multiply men upon you, all the house of Israel, all of it; and the cities shall be inhabited and the ruins rebuilt. I will multiply upon you man and beast; and they shall increase and bear young; I will make you inhabited as in former times, and do better for you than at your beginnings. Then you shall know that I am the LORD. Yes, I will cause men to walk on you, My people Israel; they shall take possession of you, and you shall be their inheritance; no more shall you bereave them of children (Ezekiel 36:8-12).

God spoke, and the dead land came alive. Later, we'll look in greater detail at the incredible recovery of the land of Israel. This barren wasteland now exports fruits and vegetables to the whole world. This is evidence of the amazing power of God's Word.

But there is more to the budding of the fig tree. Not only did God revitalize the land, but the nation was reborn. In Ezekiel 37, God's chosen people are pictured as a valley of dry, lifeless bones. If you have ever seen pictures of the survivors of the Holocaust when they were first given their freedom, it is easy to visualize the dry, dead bones metaphor. In Ezekiel, God told the prophet to prophesy,

> Behold, O My people, I will open your graves and cause you to come up from your graves, and bring you into the land of Israel. Then you shall know that I am the LORD, when I have opened your graves, O My people,

and brought you up from your graves. I will put My
Spirit in you, and you shall live, and I will place you in
your own land. Then you shall know that I, the LORD,
have spoken it and performed it (Ezekiel 37:12-14).

Again, God spoke, and this time the people came alive. God said,
"Not only will I give you life, but I will give you life on your own
soil." There is not a person on earth who has a rational explanation
for how the Jews found their way back to their land and, in 70 short
years, turned it into a world powerhouse.

Wait a minute—did you catch what I said about 70 short years?
In May of 2018, Israel celebrated 70 years of nationhood. How long
is a generation? Seventy to 100 years.

I'm going to assume that all of you who are currently reading
this book are, at the present time, alive. This means you are part of
the generation that sees Israel back in the land. You are alive to see
the nation flourish. You have seen this miraculous work of God.
Depending on your age, your great-grandparents or great-great-
grandparents didn't see that coming. In fact, for them, the restoration of Israel would have seemed a laughable impossibility. Yet here
it is—Israel's rebirth a reality in our generation.

For the first time ever, we have the church and Israel living and
thriving at the same time. When the church was born in the first
century, both Israel and the church were struggling. Then for many
years, the church was strong, but Israel was scattered. That's why
many people in the church began to worry that the prophecies
about the nation of Israel would never come to fulfillment. They
decided to help God out by saying, "We're the new Israel." No,
you're not. Stay in your lane. The church is the church, and Israel is
Israel. While the church thrived and the Jews struggled, God bided
His time, saying, "Just wait and watch what I'm going to do with

My people Israel. When I'm ready, My church is going to see My nation sprout and leaf. Then they'll know that they had better start looking up toward the skies."

We are the generation that has seen this sign.

A ROCK-SOLID NONPREDICTION

Fear not. Although I can tell you that I firmly believe that we are in the final generation, I will make no attempt to predict a date when the Lord will return. As we have seen, Jesus says, "Of that day and hour no one knows, not even the angels of heaven, but My Father only" (Matthew 24:36). Unfortunately, there are many date-predictors out there who will come up with some formula or who will receive some "new revelation." Essentially, they are saying, "Bless Your heart, Jesus. I'm sorry that You couldn't figure out the date, but I think I've got a little something that just might help You out a bit."

There's a good reason that Jesus didn't say, "I'm going to come and take you on October 27, 2030." It's because He wants you to be ready at all times. He wants you to live with expectancy. If Jesus had given us that date, then we would probably be living however we want, ignoring the kingdom of God, up until October 26. Then we would all run around screaming out the gospel message, giving our possessions away to the poor, and spending our final evening on earth in an extended prayer meeting—all so that we could show Jesus how faithful we've been. In the parable of the ten virgins, Jesus said to "watch therefore, for you know neither the day nor the hour in which the Son of Man is coming" (Matthew 25:13). The Lord could come back at any moment. We need to be ready to meet our Savior.

Israel burst back onto the international scene as an independent nation on May 14, 1948. We are now in the optimal generational timeline from that date. We are not simply in the last days, we are in the last hour of the last days. As we saw in the previous chapter, the letter to the Hebrews begins, "God, who at various times and in various ways spoke in time past to the fathers by the prophets, has *in these last days* spoken to us by His Son, whom He has appointed heir of all things, through whom also He made the worlds" (Hebrews 1:1-2). Jesus came, and the last days began. The church has been waiting in expectancy since then.

> Jesus came, and the last days began. The church has been waiting in expectancy since then.

Paul was convinced that Jesus could come and take him at any moment. When he was with the Thessalonians, he told them, "Good news everyone—you're not going to die." Then he left, and some of them died. The ones who remained wrote to him and said, "Uh, Paul, we've got a problem." So Paul wrote back:

> I do not want you to be ignorant, brethren, concerning those who have fallen asleep, lest you sorrow as others who have no hope. For if we believe that Jesus died and rose again, even so God will bring with Him those who sleep in Jesus.
>
> For this we say to you by the word of the Lord, that we who are alive and remain until the coming of the Lord will by no means precede those who are asleep. For the Lord Himself will descend from heaven with a shout, with the voice of an archangel, and with the trumpet of God. And the dead in Christ will rise first. Then we who are alive and remain shall be caught up together with them in the clouds to meet the Lord in the air. And thus we shall always be with the Lord. Therefore comfort one another with these words (1 Thessalonians 4:13-18).

Paul didn't see the budding fig tree, yet he was still expectant. How much more anticipation should we feel as part of the generation that has seen the tender branches and the sprouting leaves? As we watch and wait, we must be about our Father's business. And when times get difficult, remember what Paul said in 1 Thessalonians 4:18 and comfort each other with his words.

CHAPTER 3

SEPARATION ESCALATION

DO A LITTLE EXPERIMENT WITH ME. Think of the word *togetherness*. Let it settle in your mind for a minute. What kinds of feelings do you experience? What memories are passing through your mind? Maybe it's laughter around a family holiday dinner, or the press of warm bodies surrounding you as you held marshmallows on sticks in a campfire on a chilly mountain night. Whatever your thoughts and emotions, it's likely that they are positive. God created us as relational beings, so togetherness speaks to who we are as humans.

Now do the same experiment with the word *separation*. What emotion does that term evoke? Chances are your reaction is very different. Maybe it's the emptiness felt after a child goes off to college, or the bitterness of a failed marriage, or the pain of losing a loved one. Loneliness, sorrow, and grief often accompany separation.

When God created the heavens and the earth, it's likely that He never had separation in mind. After bringing forth the earth, the waters, and the skies, the Creator began to populate them. In the oceans, schools of fish cut through the inky deep and pods of mammals burst through the surface of the seas only to splash back down. In the air, flocks of birds migrated great distances, while swarms of insects buzzed amongst the plant life. On the ground, herds and packs and prides roamed through the grasses. This is still true today—members of a species usually gather together.

Then came man. Singular. In the midst of the many, there was one. God knew immediately that His work was not done. One final great act of creation was necessary for this work to be declared good. "And the LORD God said, 'It is not good that man should be alone; I will make him a helper comparable to him'" (Genesis 2:18). God put Adam to sleep, reached in, and pulled out a rib. Then, with a word, he transformed Adam's spare rib into a prime rib. *Togetherness* given as a gift to humanity.

Not only was there togetherness within humanity, but there was also a together-relationship between God and this pinnacle of His creation. God dwelled among men. There was perfect harmony and peace. This was what God intended; this is what God declared to be good. Unfortunately, it didn't take mankind too long to destroy the perfection of the Creator's creation.

Why didn't God stop this falling away? For humanity to have true relationship with God, we had to be given the option to fail. He couldn't have created us as robots or automatons. There is nothing meaningful or perfect about mindless love or relationship that comes from anything other than choice. So choice is what the Lord gave to us. Adam, along with all of us who descended from him, was given the option of following God or rebelling against Him. We all, like Adam, chose rebellion. The joy of togetherness was replaced by the pain of separation. From Genesis 3 to the end of Revelation, the Bible tells the story of God's perfect plan to restore the relationship that our sin shattered.

ADAM AND EVE SEPARATE FROM GOD

As mentioned above, the first separation occurred when Adam and Eve rebelled against God. Everything had been perfect up to that point. In the Garden of Eden, there was no temple. There was no need for one because God was already there. Immediately prior to the first couple admitting their sin, what do we see the Lord doing? He's walking in the garden in the cool of the day. What did that look like? Because God is spirit and thus has no flesh or bones (Luke 24:39), His walking in the garden may have involved a theophany—a physical manifestation of God that could be experienced by the senses.

Like an artist walking through his gallery, the Creator took the form of His creation and enjoyed the beauty of what His hands had made. The implication of the passage is that it was not uncommon for Adam and Eve to walk with Him. They had a relationship of companionship and fellowship.

Then came the serpent. And with him came the lies, the bite, the judgment, and the separation. "So He drove out the man; and He placed cherubim at the east of the garden of Eden, and a flaming sword which turned every way, to guard the way to the tree of life" (Genesis 3:24). First, sin created a spiritual separation. Then the Lord drove Adam and Eve out of the garden, creating a physical separation—one that He ensures is maintained by posting cherubim to guard the gates. With this disconnection from God came a disconnection from life. Notice that the tree of life was still in the garden. God is the giver of life. Where there is no relationship with Him, there is no life.

Sin is a separator. Isaiah wrote, "Behold, the LORD's hand is not shortened, that it cannot save; nor His ear heavy, that it cannot hear. But your iniquities have separated you from your God; and your sins have hidden His face from you, so that He will not hear"

(Isaiah 59:1-2). Our sins build a wall between ourselves and God. It is a barrier that we are powerless to do anything about without God's intervention.

CAIN SEPARATES FROM HIS FAMILY

The next separation in Scripture takes place when Cain parts from the rest of his family. The Lord recognized the depth to which Cain's heart had been tainted by sin, and He warned Cain against becoming easy prey to Satan. "If you do well, will you not be accepted? And if you do not do well, sin lies at the door. And its desire is for you, but you should rule over it" (Genesis 4:7). But Cain let sin rule in him, and when his jealousy became too great, he lashed out at his brother Abel. The consequence of this first murder saw Cain banished from his family and his home.

This scenario is played out over and over in today's families. When sin enters a household, separation often follows. It may begin with an affair or computer pornography. Another way it happens is through violence—physical or verbal. Sometimes alcohol or substance abuse creates the separation. When Cain killed his brother, Satan gained two victories. The first was destroying a life, and the second was destroying a family. In our modern culture, husbands and wives must be very careful because sin is lying at our doors, and its desire is for our families.

NOAH SEPARATES FROM WICKEDNESS

In the time of Noah, something new takes place. Up until now, it has been the wicked that have been separated out. Adam and Eve sinned and were separated from God. Cain sinned and was separated from his family. But in Noah's day, God gave that paradigm a 180-degree turn.

The world had become a mess. Sin was rampant. God looked at humanity and felt regret over His once-perfect creation. As a result, He made a harsh but necessary decision. "The LORD said, 'I will destroy man whom I have created from the face of the earth, both man and beast, creeping thing and birds of the air, for I am sorry that I have made them'" (Genesis 6:7). God was about to give the world a one-year bath, cleansing it from all the sin and all the sinners. Yet there was one man who stood out squeaky clean from the rest of the mud-caked rabble: "Noah found grace in the eyes of the LORD" (verse 8).

God told Noah to build a boat, fill it with animals, then hold on tight. When He closed the door to the ark, He was making a clear line of separation between what was devoted to destruction and what was blessed with salvation. Was Noah a perfect man? No. But God's grace dealt with whatever sin might have separated him from his Lord. And when the time came for the wrath of God to be executed upon the earth, the ark lifted Noah up to safety. The picture of the righteous being separated from the unrighteous world and lifted up to safety is something that we will see take place again when the Lord lifts us up to meet Him in the sky.

ABRAHAM SEPARATES FROM ALL HE KNOWS

In Genesis 12, God makes a wonderful promise to Abraham (then still Abram). He says,

> Get out of your country,
> from your family
> and from your father's house,
> to a land that I will show you.
> I will make you a great nation;
> I will bless you

and make your name great;
and you shall be a blessing.
I will bless those who bless you,
and I will curse him who curses you;
and in you all the families of the earth shall be blessed
(verses 1-3).

What an amazing blessing the Lord promised here! He committed to Abraham the gifts of posterity, greatness, blessing, and protection. Through Abraham, all people, present and future, would be blessed. But for this to take place, there was one thing Abraham had to do first. He had to separate himself from his home and his people.

Stop and think about this separation to which God was calling Abraham. How would you respond if the Lord said to you, "I have an incredible future planned for you; all you need to do is to leave everything you know and everyone you love"?

Are you ready for that kind of separation if God were to call you to it? When we follow Jesus, we must be willing to give up all for Him. Jesus said, "If anyone comes to Me and does not hate his father and mother, wife and children, brothers and sisters, yes, and his own life also, he cannot be My disciple. And whoever does not bear his cross and come after Me cannot be My disciple" (Luke 14:26-27). Of course, He is not saying that we must literally hate our family in order to be a disciple. Rather, He is talking about our heart. Our love for Jesus must be so great that our love for anyone else pales in comparison. And we must be willing to separate ourselves from anything and everything that hinders us from serving Him.

Committing ourselves to serve God and become spreaders of the gospel will sometimes cost us. At times it can lead to painful decisions. But the present and future rewards that await us when we are ready to separate ourselves from whatever drags us down will far outweigh any temporary sorrow we might experience over the things we let go of.

MOSES SEPARATES FROM EGYPT

The arrival of Moses on the scene is marked by numerous separations. First, Moses separated himself from Egypt. Born during a time of persecution, Moses was rescued by the daughter of Pharaoh and brought up in the royal household. However, he knew that he was a Hebrew and couldn't just ignore his heritage. One day when he was walking amongst his people, he came across an Egyptian who was abusing a Hebrew slave. Moses' zeal welled up inside of him and he struck and killed the Egyptian.

When this murder apparently landed Moses on the Egyptian Ten Most Wanted List, he fled the land of his upbringing and his people and went into the wilderness. It was in this rugged region that God began a 40-year process of preparing him for what was next. If Moses had remained in the comfort of the Egyptian palace, it is unlikely that he would have been ready to answer when God came calling in the burning bush. Sometimes God must separate us from the norm or the comfortable or the easy so He can prepare us to serve Him.

Next, through Moses, the Lord separated the whole Hebrew nation from Egypt. Pharaoh refused to budge through nine progressively worsening plagues. In response, God brought the tenth and most gut-wrenching attention-getter. In one night, all the firstborn of Egypt—humans and beasts—were wiped out. Heartbreaking cries resounded throughout the nation as family after family helplessly watched their children, their fathers, their grandfathers—anyone who was first from the womb—gasp and breathe their last.

This led Pharaoh to act quickly. He called for Moses and Aaron that very night and said, "Rise, go out from among my people, both you and the children of Israel. And go, serve the LORD as you have said. Also take your flocks and your herds, as you have said, and be gone; and bless me also" (Exodus 12:31-32). "Leave," he said. "Go as far away from me as you can and take all of your stuff with you. I never want to see your face again. Oh yeah, and could you bless me before you go?" God's people had been in hopeless bondage, but the Lord separated them from their captors and gave them freedom.

Continuing through the exodus, God proceeded to separate Israel from the pagan world. Egypt was a polytheistic culture with a full pantheon of gods. The Lord pulled the Hebrews out of that idol-worshipping land to establish for Himself a people who would worship Him alone. Unfortunately, you can get the Israelite out of Egypt, but it's much more difficult to get Egypt out of the Israelite.

When the people got to Sinai, Moses disappeared up the mountain for a while. The Israelites waited around, and after a few weeks, they started getting antsy. They said, "You know, it's been a month or so since this eighty-year-old walked up the mountainside without food or water. There's a good chance he's not coming back down." We'll look at this story more closely in a few chapters, but suffice it to say that one golden calf later, Moses was not a happy camper. He smashed the stone tablets God had just given him, destroyed the calf, ground up the gold, and made the people drink it.

The story doesn't end there. The people were angry. They had gotten a taste of sin and were now looking for a full meal. Moses may have been powerful, but he was facing a frenzied, lust-filled mob. He stood at the entrance to the camp and called out, "Whoever is on the Lord's side—come to me!" (Exodus 32:26).

Out of all the tribes, one stepped forward—the tribe of Levi. Moses charged them, "Thus says the LORD God of Israel: 'Let every man put his sword on his side, and go in and out from entrance to entrance throughout the camp, and let every man kill his brother, every man his companion, and every man his neighbor'" (Exodus 32:27). And that is just what they did. About 3,000 of the worst offenders were killed that day. This incident with the calf is the last time we see nationwide idol worship amongst the Hebrews until the time of the Judges, after Moses and Joshua are gone.

When the Levites stepped up to Moses' call, another separation took place. Not only were the Israelites separated from the rest of the pagan world, but the Levites also became separated from the rest of the Israelites. They were the ones who took the lead when the people needed to be cleansed of their sin, and because the Levites weren't afraid to put even their own family members to the sword in defense of God's honor, the Lord honored them.

That's why the tribe of Levi was chosen to serve as the priests of the nation. They would be the worship and sacrifice conduit between the people and their God. True separation has nothing to do with borders or race or gender or anything else. It all comes down to whether you are on the Lord's side or not. Are you separated to God, or are you separated to the world? Everyone is on one side or the other—there is no middle ground.

THE CHURCH SEPARATES FROM THE LAW AND THE WORLD

Sixteen centuries after Moses, Jesus came, and everything changed. When we last left the Jews, the Lord was separating them from a pagan culture to Judaism. Now, at the beginning of the church age, God is separating them again, but this time from traditional Judaism. Tevya can sing about tradition all he wants, but tradition is gone. No longer is relationship with God all about rules and laws. Jesus came and said that there are only two laws we need to focus on: love God and love each other. If we fulfill those commands, we'll do fine.

This was a major separation because from the Jewish people's perspective, obedience to the law was at the heart of what being a Jew was all about. Then here comes Jesus, who shifts God's paradigm from law to grace. Even Peter struggled with this transition. At one point, Peter and Paul were ministering together in Antioch. Peter was happy to eat with both Jews and Gentiles at the same time, which was forbidden by Jewish tradition. Everybody in the church was one big, happy family.

But when a group of Jews who came from the Jerusalem church saw what was going on, suddenly Peter had a change of heart. He separated himself from the Gentiles and ate at the Jews-only table. Those uncircumcised *goyim* were now too unclean to eat with. In fact, who did these Gentiles think they were, waltzing into church with their Gentile clothes and their Gentile hair and their Gentile way of speaking?

Paul, never one to keep his opinion to himself, called Peter out in front of everybody. "If you, being a Jew, live in the manner of Gentiles and not as the Jews, why do you compel Gentiles to live as Jews?" (Galatians 2:14). "We are no longer of that group that believes in the law for salvation," he tells the assembled crowd of Jews and Gentiles. He then boldly asserted, "If righteousness comes through the law, then Christ died in vain" (Galatians 2:21). Those powerful words turned the tradition paradigm on its head. This change was going to be tough, but the Jews had to learn a new way of thinking.

But it wasn't only the Jews who had to go through a major separation. The Gentile believers were faced with splitting from the pagan world in which they had lived their entire lives. In Acts 15, the growing church was faced with a question: What are we going to do with all these Gentile Christians? How Jewish do they need to become, and how Gentile can they remain?

People from both sides of the argument threw in their two shekels' worth at what has come to be known as the Jerusalem Council. Finally, James, the brother of Jesus and the head of the Jerusalem church, spoke up, saying basically what Paul had said in Antioch: "My Gentile brothers, some people have said that you need to adopt all the Jewish traditions. Ignore them. They weren't from us. We don't need more Jews; we need more Christians." That's all well and good to say, but the Gentile world was still a nasty place, so the council felt that at least a few restrictions were still in order.

After further discussion, a letter was crafted to the Gentiles and sent with Paul, Barnabas, Judas, and Silas. This letter affirmed the fellowship of Gentiles and Jews together in the Lord's church, and it concluded with these words:

> It seemed good to the Holy Spirit, and to us, to lay upon you no greater burden than these necessary things: that you abstain from things offered to idols, from blood, from things strangled, and from sexual immorality. If you keep yourselves from these, you will do well (Acts 15:28-29).

As minor as these stipulations may sound, they were actually quite major. What James forbade at the end of this missive was a large part of what made the Gentile culture the Gentile culture. So much of what the Gentiles did was about idol worship, sexual immorality, and sexually immoral idol worship. For the new Gentile believers to separate themselves from these things—as well as to turn away from foods knowingly offered to idols, as most foods were at that time—would make them stand out in their culture, and not in a positive way. Doing this could very quickly lead to ostracization and hardship. But this change was for a reason. The Gentiles had to separate themselves. They couldn't dance in two weddings at the same time.

Paul emphasized the need to separate from the idolatrous ways of the Gentiles as he stood in front of the crowd at the Areopagus in Athens. As the learned men gathered to listen, Paul told them, "God, who made the world and everything in it, since He is Lord of heaven and earth, does not dwell in temples made with hands. Nor is He worshiped with men's hands, as though He needed anything, since He gives to all life, breath, and all things" (Acts 17:24-25). In a city filled with temples, all of which were filled with idols, this was a perspective-shifting statement. "All those beautiful temples with their expensive idols? Yeah, they're worthless." Paul went on to tell his listeners that they were all one people made from one blood. God may have set the boundaries that distinguish the different people groups from each other, but that doesn't change the fact that we were all created by the same Creator.

As Paul wrapped up his speech, he told the Athenians that the same spiritual standard of separating from wickedness applies to all people. "Truly, these times of ignorance God overlooked, but now commands all men everywhere to repent, because He has appointed a day on which He will judge the world in righteousness by the Man whom He has ordained. He has given assurance of this to all by raising Him from the dead" (Acts 17:30-31). Those words "but now" are powerful. There are no more excuses. The Messiah has come. We must set ourselves apart from anything that seeks to separate us from God—whether that is Jews separating from the law, or Gentiles separating from the world.

Sometimes the cost of separation for Christ's sake can be high. It can cost marriages and children and jobs and friends. God understands that and has provided a second family for us. He did this by uniting all His children into one international body of brothers and sisters. Paul wrote, "He Himself is our peace, who has made both one, and has broken down the middle wall of separation...For through Him we both have access by one Spirit to the Father" (Ephesians 2:14,18).

Jesus broke down the walls of separation through His death on the cross. Only in Him are there no borders, no nationalities, no religion, nothing to separate us from one another. "There is neither Jew nor Greek, there is neither slave nor free, there is neither male nor female; for you are all one in Christ Jesus" (Galatians 3:28). I can't tell you the number of times I have stepped off an airplane in a country I have never visited before and been warmly greeted by a brother or sister in Christ whom I've never met but who is immediately as close as any family member I have. The reason for that is because in Christ, they truly *are* family.

God's original plan was not for separation. In Him, unity is restored.

THE CHURCH SEPARATES FROM THE WORLD

There is one more separation that we must talk about. This is the Great Separation—the one to end all separations. This is the setting apart of the church from the world. "But, Amir, didn't Jesus say, 'Be in the world, but not of the world'? Are you now saying we should separate from the world?"

First, Jesus never said this. That is how some people interpret a portion of His high priestly prayer in John 17. However, this is still a good sentiment that says we should be fully engaged with those around us while not giving in to the sinful temptations that culture throws at us.

Second, this Great Separation is not spiritual in nature, but physical. A day is going to come when the Lord will rapture His church to meet Him in the air. The result of that separation is a physical unification of believers and their Savior. From that moment onward, we will be with Him forever.

While separation was not God's original intent, it is the means He has used to work in this world through the ages. For those who think that it would be strange for the Lord to pull His people out of the world, all they need to do is to look at history. For Him to remove His people is not strange; it is His modus operandi. That is why it is so important for us as believers to be living truth and speaking truth to our families and neighbors. The church has not been separated yet—that means there is still time. As long as we are here to proclaim the gospel, people can still choose to follow God. But once we are separated from the world, the chances of those left behind finding their way to the Lord are almost gone.

By all appearances, the time is short. We must take seriously the role we've been given as ambassadors of Christ.

> Time is short. We must take seriously the role we've been given as ambassadors of Christ.

CHAPTER 4

AN EXTENDED 70 WEEKS

IT WAS A HARD LANDING, especially for his old body. Maybe 20, 30, 40 years ago he could have bounced back up. But at this age, every movement brought an ache or pain. Being tossed to the bottom of a dank, rocky pit certainly didn't help any of his ailments.

Slowly, leaning up against the wall, he slid himself to his feet. The total darkness was claustrophobic. He couldn't tell if the floor below him stretched out 6 feet or 60. One thing he did know: He was not alone in that pit. There was a soft shuffling sound around him, that of padded feet against gritty stone. Then came the first deep rumble.

"O Lord," he prayed, "take care of me down here. Protect me. My life is in your hands."

A silky, muscular body brushed against his side, knocking him back into the wall. The agitated movement was growing in intensity. The rumbles turned into snarls.

Suddenly light filled the room with such intensity that he was momentarily as blinded as he had been in the absolute darkness. As the blue dots faded from his eyes, he was able to make out a figure walking around the rocky space and gently touching the muzzles of what he now saw were a dozen or more lions surrounding him. Mesmerized, he watched this glowing man finish his task, turn his direction, and, after momentarily locking eyes with him, vanish, taking the light with him.

The rest of the night was unlike any he had spent before. He slept soundly in the blackness with the heartbeat of the beast under his head, soothing his anxious mind, and the warmth of the two magnificent creatures on either side of him more than overcoming the musty cool of the pit.

He was awakened in the morning by the voice of King Darius calling down to him, "Daniel, servant of the living God, has your God, whom you serve continually, been able to deliver you from the lions?" (Daniel 6:20). Using the great felines around him as leverage, he pushed himself to his feet and called out, "O king, live forever! My God sent His angel and shut the lions' mouths, so that they have not hurt me, because I was found innocent before Him; and also, O king, I have done no wrong before you" (verses 21-22). The king had his aged advisor removed from the pit and brought to him, and their reunion was sweet.

For many people, this is the extent of what they know about the great prophet Daniel. Pushed enough, some may remember stories about eating vegetables, interpreting dreams, and a strange party with some ghostly handwriting on a wall. But these Sunday school reminiscences would be few. Daniel was typecast early on as a lion tamer. But he was much more than that.

DANIEL AND HIS BOOK

Counting five books into the prophet section of the Old Testament (starting with Isaiah and running all the way through Malachi) will bring you to a writing unique amongst its peers. While most of these mouthpieces for God concerned themselves primarily with prophecy with a bit of historical narrative mixed in, Daniel split his book half and half.

The first six chapters are where we find some of our Sunday school lessons. Daniel was among a group of young men captured by King Nebuchadnezzar and taken back to Babylon to serve him. These chapters follow the exploits of four of the exiles—Hananiah (who was given the name Shadrach), Mishael (Meshach), Azariah (Abednego), and Daniel (Belteshazzar). Daniel's three friends end up in the spotlight in chapter 3, escaping the flames of a fiery furnace with not so much as a soot-mark. For the rest of the book, Daniel is the main star. We see him grow from exiled youth to old sage serving three world leaders of two different empires.

The second six chapters shift gears significantly. Suddenly Daniel pivots from biography and autobiography to prophecy. With the help of an angel who interpreted the strange visions and dreams he had, Daniel received direct revelation from God about future events, including the end times. This young prophet was in a unique position at a unique time. Rather than prophesying *about* the Jewish homeland *from* the Jewish homeland as most of the other prophets did, Daniel was in a foreign country seeing visions concerning God's plans for the rest of the world.

ISRAEL IN TIME-OUT

In Daniel's time, Israel was being disciplined. Daniel wasn't responsible for his exile situation in a foreign country; he was caught up in the punishment for the sins that had been committed by the generations preceding him. Essentially the nation was in what could be considered a national time-out. "If you can't follow the rules, young man, then you go sit in the corner until I tell you it's time to come out." The corner was Babylon, and the length of time turned out to be 70 years.

What had the Israelites done to get this punishment? Well, name it. If God had said, "Don't do it," then chances are the Israelites had done it. However, this specific temporary banishment was closely tied to one sin in particular. Just like God has a plan for His people, He has a plan for His land. He knows what is needed for the protection of its soil and the inherent nutrients. If you overfarm a plot of land, your crops will suffer. Thus, it is important to occasionally give the ground rest.

God's plan for resting the land coincided with His plan for resting the people. The Israelites were to consider every seventh day a Sabbath day to rest their bodies. In the same way, God designated every seventh year to be a Sabbath year to rest the soil. Logically, this made sense. Practically, it was much more difficult to do. Sabbath years took planning, and, more than that, they took faith:

> If you say, "What shall we eat in the seventh year, since we shall not sow nor gather in our produce?" Then I will command My blessing on you in the sixth year, and it will bring forth produce enough for three years. And you shall sow in the eighth year, and eat old produce until the ninth year; until its produce comes in, you shall eat of the old harvest (Leviticus 25:20-22).

God's promise was that He would give such a huge harvest in year six that the people would be eating it until the new crops were harvested in year nine.

As with so many of God's commands, the blessing of obedience is balanced with the curse of disobedience. If the Israelites decided to ignore God's rules regarding the land Sabbath, He promised the following:

> I will bring the land to desolation, and your enemies who dwell in it shall be astonished at it. I will scatter you among the nations and draw out a sword after you; your land shall be desolate and your cities waste. Then the land shall enjoy its sabbaths as long as it lies desolate and you are in your enemies' land; then the land shall rest and enjoy its sabbaths. As long as it lies desolate it shall rest—for the time it did not rest on your sabbaths when you dwelt in it (Leviticus 26:32-35).

The land would have its Sabbaths one way or another. If the Israelites refused to let the land rest, the Lord would refuse the Israelites the land until the Sabbaths were completed.

For 490 years, the land Sabbaths were ignored. Divide 490 years by 7 (or 1 Sabbath year every 7 years), and you are left with 70. That is the number of years that God designated for the exile of the people of Judah:

> Those who escaped from the sword he carried away to Babylon, where they became servants to him and his sons until the rule of the kingdom of Persia, to fulfill the word of the LORD by the mouth of Jeremiah, until the land had enjoyed her Sabbaths. As long as she lay desolate she kept Sabbath, to fulfill seventy years (2 Chronicles 36:20-21).

When God asks us to do something, it's going to get done. We can choose the easy way or the hard way. Why do we, along with the Israelites, so often choose the hard way?

Daniel was caught up in this Sabbath-year exile. However, even though he was taken from his land for a nationwide sin, he himself was still a follower of God and a student of the Scriptures. In his time, God's people didn't have the full Bible yet; he and others were still writing it. It would have been difficult for him to do an in-depth interpretive analysis of Daniel 9 when he was still scratching out chapter 6. Also, what Scriptures God had already given to them were written on scrolls and kept in synagogues. During the early part of the Babylonian exile, God's written Word was as hard to come by in Babylon as a bacon cheeseburger in Jerusalem. Yet Daniel was still well versed in God's words.

At this time, the Israelites were very much an illiterate, oral culture. People didn't walk around with their own personal scrolls in a zip-up scroll cover loaded with Post-it notes and highlighter pens. They learned God's Word by hearing it read or chanted to them. As they heard the words over and over, they would try to memorize it—often by reciting or chanting along.

This is how Daniel was able to know the length of the Jewish exile as spoken through the prophet Jeremiah:

> In the first year of Darius the son of Ahasuerus, of the lineage of the Medes, who was made king over the realm of the Chaldeans—in the first year of his reign I, Daniel, understood by the books the number of the years specified by the word of the Lord through Jeremiah the prophet, that He would accomplish seventy years in the desolations of Jerusalem (Daniel 9:1-2).

God will fulfill His promises in His time and in His way, 100 percent of the time.

Daniel, now quite old and under a new Persian empire, then prayed, in essence, "Okay, Lord, I've been counting years, and it's getting time to forgive us and send us back home according to Your promise."

When we pray, God hears. When the Lord makes a promise, we can hold Him to it. When we pray a reminder to Him, as Daniel did, it is not because we think He may have forgotten. He's not looking at His calendar thinking, *I know I circled that date for a reason.* When we remind God of His promises, it is a statement of faith on our part. We are affirming that He is a God who always follows through with His commitments. He will fulfill His promises in His time and in His way, 100 percent of the time.

THE APOCALYPSE OF DANIEL

Most often with prophecy, we are not given insight into the communication process between God and the prophet. Instead, we simply read the words that the Lord somehow transferred to His spokesman. Occasionally, the method of communication and the message itself are so intertwined that the Holy Spirit opens the methodological door. The book of Daniel is one such case.

The second half of Daniel's letter is what we would call apocalyptic literature. *Apocalypse* means "revelation" or "disclosure," and the word centers on God's coming judgment of the world and the ultimate fulfilling of His end-time plans for all mankind.[1] The book of Revelation is another great example of apocalyptic literature in the Bible.

However, Daniel can also be loosely seen as revelatory or apocalyptic in the sense that we the readers get to watch the prophecy being revealed. In chapter 7, Daniel is sleeping on his bed when his dreams and a heavenly vision merge and he clearly sees four great beasts coming up out of the waters. The prophet then narrates to us the violent and bloody actions of these creatures, the exploits of one of the horns belonging to the fourth beast, and an awe-inspiring view of the Ancient of Days taking a seat on His throne. Understandably confused at what was taking place, Daniel approached one of those "who stood by" and asked what in the world he was watching (verse 16). This man proceeded to give Daniel a detailed commentary on the action.

In the next chapter, Daniel has another vision. In this one, he is standing beside a canal watching as a ram and a goat get into a scuffle, which the goat gets the best of. Then there is more strange horn action that takes place, which greatly confuses Daniel. This time, the angel Gabriel is sent to explain the vision. This great archangel must have been awesome to behold, because Daniel immediately drops to the ground and lays himself out prostrate. Gabriel raises Daniel to his feet, then proceeds to explain this vision.

In all of Scripture, there are only three angels who are identified to us by name—Gabriel, Michael, and Lucifer. Gabriel is a messenger. He appears five times in the Bible; two of those occurrences are here in Daniel. This is the same mighty archangel who delivers the good news to two sets of soon-to-be parents. First, he visits the elderly priest Zechariah in the temple and announces God's promise to bring a son to him and his wife, who had been childless. This child would be named John and would one day baptize the Messiah. He also visits the engaged couple Mary and Joseph, separately, to share the miraculous news that the Holy Spirit was going to place a child in Mary's womb, even though she was a virgin. This child would be the literal Immanuel—"God with us."

Returning to the vision in Daniel 9, we find that Gabriel traveled a long way to bring Daniel a special message:

> While I was speaking, praying, and confessing my sin and the sin of my people Israel, and presenting my supplication before the LORD my God for the holy mountain of my God, yes, while I was speaking in prayer, the man Gabriel, whom I had seen in the vision at the beginning, being caused to fly swiftly, reached me about the time of the evening offering. And he informed me, and talked with me, and said, "O Daniel, I have now come forth to give you skill to understand" (Daniel 9:20-22).

Gabriel begins his message by saying, "O Daniel." Isn't it good that God knows us by name? He didn't send Gabriel out and say, "Gabe, see that guy down there? I'm not exactly sure who he is, but he seems to be a pretty good writer. Go grab a name from him, then give him a message from Me." Gabriel knew exactly who Daniel was because God knew exactly who Daniel was. In the same way, He knows exactly who each and every one of us is.

Gabriel is tasked with the errand of bringing "skill to understand." Another way to translate those words is "insight and understanding." Whose insight and understanding is he going to give? His own? Remember, he is just the messenger. The insight and understanding is all God's. It's as if the Lord hands a scroll to Gabriel and says, "Here, take this to Daniel so that he will read it and understand what I want him to know."

Next we hear something wonderful. Gabriel says, "At the beginning of your supplications the command went out, and I have come to tell you, for you are greatly beloved; therefore consider the matter, and understand the vision" (verse 23). From the moment Daniel started praying, God began answering. The Lord didn't insist on delaying until the praise, confession, and thanksgiving portion of the prayer were done. He didn't wait until Daniel said, "Amen" before He would consider the intercession. The instant that Daniel uttered his first syllable, God's command went to Gabriel to bring a message and understanding to His prophet. Our God, who knows the words we are going to say even before we say them, is less concerned about what comes out of our mouths than what is in our hearts.

DANIEL'S SEVENTY WEEKS

What message is Gabriel tasked with bringing? He begins, "Seventy weeks are determined for your people and for your holy city" (verse 24). Remember what we read in the beginning of Daniel 9? In the first two verses, Daniel prays to God about the 70 years of exile that God had proclaimed through the prophet Jeremiah. As Daniel pleads to the Lord about the 70-year exile, God sends him a message about something much bigger—70 weeks. Now, you may be saying, "Amir, I am no math genius. But I'm pretty sure that 70 years is longer than 70 weeks." Normally you would be correct. But the weeks Gabriel talks about are not made up of seven days, but seven years. So, the 70 weeks actually refers to a period of 490 years—70 x 7.

Who are these supersized 70 weeks for? Gabriel says that they are for Daniel's "people and for your holy city." Who are Daniel's people? Israel. What is the holy city? Jerusalem. Even though Daniel is in exile far away from his homeland, the Lord brings him a message about Jerusalem and the Jews. Gabriel reports:

> Seventy weeks are determined
> for your people and for your holy city,
> to finish the transgression,
> to make an end of sins,
> to make reconciliation for iniquity,
> to bring in everlasting righteousness,
> to seal up vision and prophecy,
> and to anoint the Most Holy.
> Know therefore and understand,
> that from the going forth of the command
> to restore and build Jerusalem
> until Messiah the Prince,
> there shall be seven weeks and sixty-two weeks;
> the street shall be built again, and the wall,
> even in troublesome times.
> and after the sixty-two weeks
> Messiah shall be cut off, but not for Himself;

and the people of the prince who is to come
shall destroy the city and the sanctuary.
The end of it shall be with a flood (Daniel 9:24-26).

There are two series of weeks listed here—7 weeks and 62 weeks. The first 7 weeks are for the rebuilding of Jerusalem. That's 7 x 7, or 49 years, to put the city back in order. Then 62 more weeks will pass: 7 x 62 = 434 years. After that, something magnificent will take place—the Messiah will come. But before you get too excited about the Messiah's arrival, realize that His coming will not be for long. No sooner will He arrive than He will quickly be cut off.

A 69-week (483 year) countdown is given for the advent of the Messiah, but 69 weeks from when? At what moment should Daniel press the start button on the stopwatch? In verse 25 of the above passage, God gives the answer: "Know therefore and understand, that from the going forth of the command to restore and build Jerusalem…" When the nation is told to go back and rebuild the city, that is when the countdown begins.

That brings us to the next question: When were the Jews told to go back and rebuild Jerusalem? People have pointed to several different dates. In 536 BC, King Cyrus of the Persians—the empire that defeated the Babylonians and now ruled the Jews—issued a command: "Thus says Cyrus king of Persia: All the kingdoms of the earth the LORD God of heaven has given me. And He has commanded me to build Him a house at Jerusalem which is in Judah" (Ezra 1:2).

Cyrus allowed the Jews to return to Jerusalem for the express purpose of building their temple. Then in 519 BC, when the Jews were being harassed during their building efforts, King Darius I followed up Cyrus's command with one of his own. The Jews were to continue the work of rebuilding, and woe to anyone who might hinder them (Ezra 6:3-12). And finally, in 448 BC, Artaxerxes I issued a declaration commanding the beautification of the temple (Ezra 7:11-26).

Which of these proclamations should serve as the starting date? None of them. Though three different decrees were given, none of them have to do with the city. Rather, they are all focused on the temple.

There is only one proclamation that was issued for the rebuilding of Jerusalem itself, and to find this we need to read past Ezra to the book of Nehemiah. Nehemiah was the cupbearer for King Artaxerxes I. His heart had been heavy for some time as he thought of Jerusalem, the holy city of God, having no gates and walls. This great capital was now a shadow of its former glory. He had prayed and fasted, pleading with the Lord to show His mercy.

As the cupbearer to the king, Nehemiah had one very important job to do: sip the king's wine. Now, if that doesn't sound like a half-bad deal for you, then you don't yet understand the reason for the sipping. The king always had a target on his back, and one prime way assassins could get to the monarch was through poison. The cupbearer's job was to bring the king his wine, sip it in his royal presence, and if he didn't drop dead, then he would give the king his cup. This taste-testing was to be done with a smile on the cupbearer's face.

But there came a day when Nehemiah slipped up. His mind was so weighed down by the situation in Jerusalem that he forgot to turn his frown upside down. King Artaxerxes called him out on it.

> "Why is your face sad, since you are not sick? This is nothing but sorrow of heart."
>
> So I became dreadfully afraid, and said to the king, "May the king live forever! Why should my face not be sad, when the city, the place of my fathers' tombs, lies waste, and its gates are burned with fire?"

Then the king said to me, "What do you request?"

So I prayed to the God of heaven. And I said to the king, "If it pleases the king, and if your servant has found favor in your sight, I ask that you send me to Judah, to the city of my fathers' tombs, that I may rebuild it."

Then the king said to me (the queen also sitting beside him), "How long will your journey be? And when will you return?" So it pleased the king to send me; and I set him a time (Nehemiah 2:2-6).

For the first time, the command was given to go back to Jerusalem to build not the temple, but the city itself. Nehemiah said, "It came to pass in the month of Nisan, in the twentieth year of King Artaxerxes" (Nehemiah 2:1). The month was Nisan, and the year was 445 BC. This was the moment of the prophecy; this was the start of the countdown.

GETTING MATHEMATICAL

Tick…tick…tick…

Time began to pass. On the countdown clock was 69 weeks, or 483 years (69 x 7), until the world would experience the glorious work of the promised Messiah.

"Amir, I told you this was all fuzzy math. I can add numbers, and 483 years from 445 BC brings us to AD 38. Jesus had already ascended into heaven well before that date." Very true, and I applaud your arithmetic skills. The problem is that while your numbers are right, your years are wrong. The Jewish year differs from the standard 365-day Gregorian calendar. Because Israel follows a lunar calendar, their year has only 360 days.

Okay, strap in—we're about to get mathematical. Sixty-nine weeks times 7 lunar years equals 483 lunar years, and 483 lunar years times 360 days equals 173,880 days. Applying this to our solar calendar requires another step. Take the 173,880 days, divide that by 365 days per solar year, and you end up with 476 solar years.

If your mind is swimming with numbers, don't worry—there is only one more easy addition problem left. The month of Nisan in 445 BC plus 476 solar years brings us right to Palm Sunday AD 31—the very moment when a certain Savior of mankind was riding into Jerusalem on the back of a donkey. Feel free to take a moment to say "Hallelujah" and "Praise the Lord" before you read on.

When Daniel lifted up his prayer, he wanted a little insight about what was going to happen to the exiled people of Israel. God, however, gave Daniel a much bigger picture of what would happen in the future. Daniel asked God about the restoration of the Jews, and God told him about the salvation of mankind.

THE MISSING SEVENTIETH WEEK

Where are we now in the 70-week timeline that Daniel received from the Lord? There were two periods of time that Daniel dealt with. The first was the 7 and 62. As we've seen, this period was about the coming of the Messiah, His crucifixion, and His being cut off. But there is a seventieth week. Keep in mind that while Daniel was brilliant for his time, he did not have access to a complete perspective of what was to come. Gabriel never attended the heavenly Baptist seminary. They both knew only what God had revealed through His message. They could see only the time frame God allowed them to see.

Clarence Larkin, an early twentieth-century pastor and Bible teacher, compared this limited sight line of prophecy to two mountains.[2] If you have ever been hiking in a mountain range, you likely will have experienced a certain optical illusion. As you are walking up the trail, you see two mountains in front of you—a slightly larger one situated immediately behind the other. Thinking it won't take much to scale both rises, you set off up the first. However, when you get to the top, you make a heart-sinking discovery. That second peak that looked like it was immediately behind the first is actually way off in the distance. Between the two mountains is a long valley that you never knew was there. It had been there the whole time, but you couldn't see it because it wasn't in your sight line.

In God's prophetic message of the 70 weeks, Daniel essentially defines two mountain peaks of time. The first includes the 69 weeks, and it is right in front of him. The second is the seventieth week and is a long way off. In between the two peaks is a long valley of time not included in the 70 weeks. Daniel doesn't mention the valley because it is beyond the sight line that God gave to him. This is where those who study Daniel's prophecy can get confused. As we read, we climb to the top of week 69 with him, fully expecting to move right on to 70. However, when we get to the top, week 70 isn't there.

Bible interpreters often take one of two paths to finding the missing week. Some take an allegorical approach and try to force that final week into the destruction of Jerusalem in the year AD 70. Others simply say there must be something wrong in the overall timing and interpretation of Daniel's message. Neither course of action is accurate, needed, or warranted.

If we just lift our eyes up from the top of Mount 69, we can clearly see the peak of Mount 70 in the distance. To get there is simply a matter of walking through the valley of time. As we hike down the far side of the first mountain, we enter the church era. Here we find the church and the Holy Spirit working together to spread the truth of the gospel. The Holy Spirit is always powerfully alongside us, lighting our trail as we walk. The path of the church, however, is sadly inconsistent. Sometimes it is paved and smooth. Other times it is cracked and falling apart. Through it all, though, with the Holy Spirit's help, we are able to keep moving forward.

When we reach the base of the second mountain, the path of the church abruptly ends. This is the rapture, when the church and the Holy Spirit are pulled from the earth. It is at this time that God's focus turns back upon Israel. The path gets rough as we walk up this second mountain. This is the time of Jacob's trouble, when God's wrath is being poured out upon the world and discipline is being meted out to the Jews. When we finally arrive at the summit, we will witness the Lord's feet setting down on the Mount of Olives. This momentous event will usher in the great revival promised by Paul in Romans 11:26: "And so all Israel will be saved."

The valley between Mount 69 and Mount 70 belongs to the church; the mountains themselves belong to Israel. Daniel 9 lists six reasons for these prophesied 70 weeks—each one starting with the word *to*.

> Seventy weeks are determined
> for your people and for your holy city,
> to finish the transgression,
> to make an end of sins,
> to make reconciliation for iniquity,
> to bring in everlasting righteousness,
> to seal up vision and prophecy,
> and to anoint the Most Holy (Daniel 9:24).

At His first coming, Jesus accomplished the first three of these great tasks. He finished transgression, made an end of sins, and made reconciliation for iniquity. All of these were done on the cross. When Jesus sacrificed Himself, He paid for our sins and reconciled us to God. "God demonstrates His own love toward us, in that while we were still sinners, Christ died for us...For if when we were enemies we were reconciled to God through the death of His Son, much more, having been reconciled, we shall be saved by His life" (Romans 5:8,10). Through faith in Jesus' work on the cross, we are made right with our Father and are now at peace with Him.

The last three tasks will be completed when Jesus returns. As the King of kings ruling on earth, He will bring in everlasting righteousness. He Himself will be the fulfillment of visions and prophecies, and the completion of them. Why would the Lord need to communicate through visions and prophecies when He Himself is dwelling among mankind? Finally, Jesus Christ will return as the anointed Most Holy one. Not only will He return as the King of kings, but as the Lord of lords.

The day of the seventieth week is approaching. God is going to deal once again with Israel. The valley between the peaks was a desert for the Jews. But then came 1948, and suddenly Israel was back home. God has brought Israel back—and now we are waiting for Him to pour out His Spirit upon the Jewish people. What a glorious day it will be when we see mass repentance and reconciliation between the Lord and His chosen nation! Lift up your eyes— the base of the mountain is almost at our feet, and the path of the church is nearing the end.

CHAPTER 5

THE LONG SHADOW
OF THE PASSOVER

IN APRIL 2012, AT THE COACHELLA VALLEY Music and Arts Festival, rapper Tupac Shakur took the stage. What was unique about this live performance was that Tupac was not actually alive. Sixteen years earlier, this gangster rapper had been killed in a drive-by shooting in Las Vegas, Nevada. Yet here he was on stage performing before an audience of thousands of screaming fans.

Obviously, Tupac was not actually there. Even in the world of gangster rap, carting a dead body out onto a stage would likely be looked upon as a bit extreme. Instead, what the audience was watching was a brilliant blend of projectors, mirrors, foil screens, and a lot of math.[1] Tupac was a hologram. For the fans, the excitement of seeing one of their musical heroes was enough to cause them to forget that what they were looking at was not real. No matter what their eyes were telling them, Tupac was still dead. When the performance was over and the projector was switched off, their idol went back to just being an old memory for a passing generation.

SHADOW VS. SUBSTANCE

In the Bible, something very similar takes place. Through His prophets and writers, the Lord often used shadows to represent something of substance—sort of like ancient literary holograms that represent something or someone real. The writer of Hebrews tells us that many years ago there was an earthly sanctuary set up for sacrifices offered to the Lord. He gives a brief tour, pointing out the lampstand, the table, and the showbread. Pulling back the sacred curtain, he leads us into the Holy of Holies, "which had the golden censer and the ark of the covenant overlaid on all sides with gold, in which were the golden pot that had the manna, Aaron's rod that budded, and the tablets of the covenant; and above it were the cherubim of glory overshadowing the mercy seat" (Hebrews 9:4-5). These were all created so that the priests could perform their ritual duties, the capstone of which was the high priest making the annual atonement sacrifice for the sins of the people.

But as wonderful as this first temple and sacrificial system were, we are told that they were only "symbolic for the present time" (verse 9). They were only the shadow—an illustration of a greater reality. That greater reality is found in the heavenly temple and the sacrifice of Jesus Christ:

> Christ came as High Priest of the good things to come, with the greater and more perfect tabernacle not made with hands, that is, not of this creation. Not with the blood of goats and calves, but with His own blood He entered the Most Holy Place once for all, having obtained eternal redemption (verses 11-12).

This shadow/substance pairing is found throughout Scripture. In fact, it could be said that it is the essence of biblical prophecy. Sometimes the shadow is simply given in a prophetic word: "You, Bethlehem Ephrathah, though you are little among the thousands of Judah, yet out of you shall come forth to Me the One to be Ruler in Israel, whose goings forth are from of old, from everlasting" (Micah 5:2). This declaration presages the wonderful reality of Jesus the Messiah being born in the unassuming town of Bethlehem.

Sometimes the shadow is disclosed in an event. In the book of Isaiah, a sign is given to evil King Ahaz of Judah that his small nation will not be destroyed by the combined armies of Aram and Israel:

> Behold, the virgin shall conceive and bear a Son, and shall call His name Immanuel. Curds and honey He shall eat, that He may know to refuse the evil and choose the good. For before the Child shall know to refuse the evil and choose the good, the land that you dread will be forsaken by both her kings (Isaiah 7:14-16).

The shadow of God's redemption is seen when this woman who was unmarried at the time of this prophecy gives birth to a son, and the Lord follows up the birth with salvation for the nation of Judah. The substance is revealed 700 years later, when a virgin gives birth to a son who is the true Immanuel—God with us. And rather than bringing about the salvation of a nation, this Child will be used by the Father to bring about the salvation of the world.

THE SHADOW OF THE FEASTS

There is a growing trend in the Christian church to celebrate the feasts of the Old Testament. Many churches will gather together over a seder meal around Easter. Others follow the full Jewish calendar, seeing in Scripture a mandate for the festivals to be carried out by today's believers. One such denomination is the Living Church of God, which has around 10,000 members spread over six continents. Roderick Meredith, the founder of the church, states,

> These days were clearly commanded in the Old Testament, and their observance by Christ and the Apostles in the New Testament certainly ratifies them for the Christian Church. True Christians are to keep holy the days God made holy. And we are to follow the example of Jesus and the original Apostles in so doing.[2]

The problem with this viewpoint is that Pastor Meredith and others who adopt his position are focused on the shadow and not the substance.

When I walk in the sun, I will see my shadow. If you don't see your shadow when you walk in sunshine, you may want to go to a doctor and get that checked out—you are likely either a vampire or you don't really exist. Sometimes my shadow can be big and impressive; other times it can be barely discernible. But no matter the size, I can guarantee that if you see my shadow, then the real me is nearby. The shadow is a forerunner of the genuine article. Once the real deal is here, why focus on the shadow anymore? Paul tells us, "Let no one judge you in food or in drink, or regarding a festival or a new moon or sabbaths, which are a shadow of things to come, but the substance is of Christ" (Colossians 2:16-17). The feasts are a shadow; the substance is Christ. The feasts have done their job; let's now focus on the real thing.

> The feasts are a shadow; the substance is Christ. The feasts have done their job; let's now focus on the real thing.

While it is not necessary to celebrate the feasts anymore because they are simply the shadow, it is still important to study them. In the feasts, we can see God's great plan of redemption for the world played out. God is an amazing storyteller. Sometimes He uses history to tell His story, sometimes parables, sometimes prophecy. In the feasts of the Old Testament, we find God at His storytelling best.

For 400 years, God's chosen people were slaves in Egypt. They lived a harsh life filled with hard work and cruelty. The people cried out to God, and God heard them. From a burning bush, the Lord told Moses,

> I have surely seen the oppression of My people who are in Egypt, and have heard their cry because of their taskmasters, for I know their sorrows. So I have come down to deliver them out of the hand of the Egyptians, and to bring them up from that land to a good and large land, to a land flowing with milk and honey (Exodus 3:7-8).

Moses obediently went down to Egypt, and havoc soon followed.

Through blood and bugs and weather and death, God finally convinced Pharaoh to let His people go. As soon as this release took place, God charged Moses with creating a calendar. "Now the LORD spoke to Moses and Aaron in the land of Egypt, saying, 'This month shall be your beginning of months; it shall be the first month of the year to you'" (Exodus 12:1-2). This calendar would be based on a number of symbols seen in the actions that God was about to carry out. So that the people would remember these events and celebrate God's intervention, feasts were to be celebrated year after year. The exodus from Egypt, which eventually was expanded into a 40-year wandering, was a journey that God intended His people to journal.

Out of this wilderness time would come the seven festivals that make up the Jewish calendar—Passover, the Feast of Unleavened Bread, the Feast of Firstfruits, the Feast of Weeks (or Pentecost), the Feast of Trumpets, the Day of Atonement, and the Feast of Tabernacles. Each festival meant something important to the Israelites—a special time mandated by God. Yet they are all only shadows of a future and greater substance to be revealed in the Lord's time and in His way.

THE BEGINNING OF THE PASSOVER

The inaugural feast and the beginning of the calendar was initiated on the horrific night that saw the blood of the firstborn sons and beasts shed across Egypt. This was a message so extreme that it finally broke Pharaoh's stubborn will. Calling Moses and Aaron to him in the middle of the night, he commanded them, "Rise, go out from among my people, both you and the children of Israel" (Exodus 12:31). The Hebrews were free; their new life had begun. This freedom was a shadow of what God had planned for not just one nation, but for the world.

The Passover remembrance originated with a command to gather family together and select a lamb:

> Speak to all the congregation of Israel, saying: "On the tenth of this month every man shall take for himself a lamb, according to the house of his father, a lamb for a household...Your lamb shall be without blemish, a male of the first year. You may take it from the sheep or from the goats. Now you shall keep it until the fourteenth day of the same month. Then the whole assembly of the congregation of Israel shall kill it at twilight. And they shall take some of the blood and put it on the two doorposts and on the lintel of the houses where they eat it" (Exodus 12:3,5-7).

Notice the timing of this. The lamb was to be selected on the tenth of the month and brought into the household. Then for the next four days, they were to treat the lamb as if it were a part of the family. The children could pet it and play with it and love on it. Four days is long enough for this little lamb to shift from barnyard animal to family member.

After the time of bonding, they were to take that cute, fluffy little lamb outside and slaughter it so that its blood could be sprinkled on the doorposts of the house with a branch of hyssop. Why would God take a family through the process of bonding with a baby sheep only to have them gruesomely butcher it and spread its blood around? God wanted to make a point to His people and to have their feelings touched by the process. He wanted this to be more than just a ritual with one of their livestock. There is a price to pay when it comes to shedding blood—a price that is paid from the heart, not just the wallet.

On the night that the blood was sprinkled, the Lord came. Wherever He saw blood, He passed by. Wherever He didn't, He left behind death. Notice that this wasn't about Jew versus Egyptian, chosen versus unchosen, slave versus free—it was all about the blood. The importance of the blood can't be overstated. The Israelites weren't saved by virtue of the fact that they were God's chosen people. They were saved by the blood on their doorposts. If any of them had neglected the command to put the blood on their doors, the angel would have destroyed the Hebrew firstborn along with the firstborn Egyptians.

Later during the wilderness wanderings, when the ark of the covenant was made, the eyes of the cherubim on top of the ark were directed toward the mercy seat, where the blood was sprinkled for the atonement of the sins of the nation. God sees the blood. And the blood of the sacrificial lamb will free people from judgment and death, no matter who they are.

SHADOW AND SUBSTANCE IN THE PASSOVER

That sprinkled blood is the shadow. We learn of the substance from the lips of John the Baptist, the forerunner of Christ. As his name would indicate, John was down by the river baptizing people. Then one day, he looked up and "saw Jesus coming toward him, and said, 'Behold! The Lamb of God who takes away the sin of the world!'" (John 1:29). Of all the names that John could have used to point to the long-awaited Messiah, why did John choose that one? The name *Lion of Judah* would have been a much stronger, more appropriate choice for starting a great messianic movement. But John saw in Jesus an even more powerful and purposeful role. He saw in Jesus that which every Jew would have in his or her mind at Passover: that sacrificial lamb they had brought into their homes, grown to love, and then slaughtered—its blood being poured out for the salvation of all who take refuge under it.

The shadow of the Passover was fulfilled in the substance of Jesus. Paul wrote, "Indeed Christ, our Passover, was sacrificed for us" (1 Corinthians 5:7). That which was given to Israel all those years ago still applies to us today, and to an even greater degree. It is Christ's blood on the doorposts of our hearts that will cause death to pass us by. But the death we are now avoiding is not a physical death, but a spiritual one—an eternity separated from God.

There is a second shadow that we find in the institution of Passover. When leaving Egypt on a long journey, a traveler is going to need some food. The departure time for the Jewish people was fairly sudden and certainly unexpected after Pharaoh had reneged on his promises time after time. Because of the rush, there was no time for the Hebrews to whip up some New York-style bagels. A nice, crusty sourdough bread was definitely out of the question. Why? There was no time for the yeast to do its business. No yeast, no rise. No rise, no leavened bread.

As a result of the short time frame for their departure, the Hebrews went with the food that they had time for. They took some flour, mixed it with water, and threw it into the oven. While it cooked, the surface of the oven baked brown stripes into the bread. Those tending the oven would pierce the dough to keep it from bubbling and rising. After a short bake time, what emerged was a flat bread—food designed less for enjoyment and more for meeting a physical need.

To ensure that future generations remembered the haste with which the Hebrews fled, the Lord instituted the Feast of Unleavened Bread to accompany Passover.

> On the fourteenth day of the first month at twilight is the Lord's Passover. And on the fifteenth day of the same month is the Feast of Unleavened Bread to the Lord; seven days you must eat unleavened bread. On the first day you shall have a holy convocation; you shall do no customary work on it. But you shall offer an offering made by fire to the Lord for seven days. The seventh day shall be a holy convocation; you shall do no customary work on it (Leviticus 23:5-8).

For seven days they were commanded to eat this unleavened flat bread. Why seven days? This was a precautionary measure. Seven days are long enough to ensure that absolutely no leaven had slipped into the dough.

The substance to the shadow of unleavened bread is again seen in 1 Corinthians 5:7. Paul commanded us to "purge out the old leaven, that you may be a new lump, since you truly are unleavened." What is the leaven that we are purging? Sin. Paul went on to write, "Therefore let us keep the feast, not with old leaven, nor with the leaven of malice and wickedness, but with the unleavened bread of sincerity and truth" (verse 8). When we are forgiven of our sins, we become unleavened—pure and holy before God.

Who is our ultimate example of the unleavened life? It is Jesus. He lived here on this earth long enough for all to see that there was no leaven in Him. "We do not have a High Priest who cannot sympathize with our weaknesses, but was in all points tempted as we are, yet without sin" (Hebrews 4:15). At the Last Supper, Jesus took the unleavened bread of the Passover and He broke it. He said, "This is My body which is given for you; do this in remembrance of Me" (Luke 22:19). The blood of the Passover lamb is the shadow of the sacrifice Christ would make to take away our sins, and the bread purified of the leaven sees its fulfillment in the sinless perfection of the Bread of Life.

The sacrifice of Jesus Christ is what makes all the difference for our eternity. Without the acceptance of Jesus Christ and the forgiveness that comes through His sacrifice, the view of the day approaching will look very much like the light from an oncoming train. However, by making Jesus our Savior and our Lord, we can look forward to seeing our soon-returning Messiah. We know that the moment we meet Him in the air will be the beginning of an eternity in His glorious presence.

CHAPTER 6

THE LONG SHADOW OF THE OTHER FEASTS

THE PASSOVER WAS THE FIRST FEAST INSTITUTED, and it made a huge impact. It reminded the Hebrews of God's power and faithfulness, united them together as one people, and provided an opportunity for national worship. Although Passover was the first of the feasts, it was certainly not the last. Six more feasts were to follow—each one with its own rituals and its own purpose. And, like Passover, each of the other feasts had both a shadow component and the ultimate substance.

THE FEAST OF FIRSTFRUITS

The day following Passover, the priests gathered together baskets of grain. After roasting the kernels, they coarsely ground them and dumped the rough flour into a large bowl. Pouring in olive oil, they mixed the flour into an aromatic paste. One of the priests would then take this bowl and lift it up before God in recognition that the harvest had come from Him.[1] He is the One who gave the seed to plant; He is the One who gave the rain to water the seed; He is the One who caused the plant to grow.

This is the ritual that took place for the Feast of the Firstfruits. The Lord told Moses,

> Speak to the children of Israel, and say to them: "When you come into the land which I give to you, and reap its harvest, then you shall bring a sheaf of the firstfruits of your harvest to the priest. He shall wave the sheaf before the LORD, to be accepted on your behalf; on the day after the Sabbath the priest shall wave it. And you shall offer on that day, when you wave the sheaf, a male lamb of the first year, without blemish, as a burnt offering to the LORD. Its grain offering shall be two-tenths of an ephah of fine flour mixed with oil, an offering made by fire to the LORD, for a sweet aroma; and its drink offering shall be of wine, one-fourth of a hin. You shall eat neither bread nor parched grain nor fresh grain until the same day that you have brought an offering to your God; it shall be a statute forever throughout your generations in all your dwellings" (Leviticus 23:10-14).

"But, Amir, when I looked up this feast in my biblical encyclopedia, there was a picture of a priest happily waving a freshly cut bundle of grain before the Lord. He wasn't lifting up some bowl of smelly paste." The confusion arises in the translation of the word "sheaf," which in the original Hebrew text is *omer*. An *omer* is a unit of measurement thought to be equivalent to an amount of grain that needs bundling.[2] This would work out to be about three to three-and-a-half liters. When we read the word "sheaf" in this context, it is speaking of an amount of grain waved as opposed to the form of that waving grain.

This acknowledgment of God's blessing of the firstfruits took place the day after the Sabbath. In Hebrew, each day of the week is numbered—first day, second day, third day—all up to the last day of the week, which is Shabbat. So the day after the Sabbath is first day, or Sunday.

The yearly Sunday waving of God's provision was a great opportunity for the Israelites to thank and praise the Lord. However, this was only a shadow of an even greater reality that was, again, found in Christ. Matthew described the events of another celebration of firstfruits:

> Now after the Sabbath, as the first day of the week began to dawn, Mary Magdalene and the other Mary came to see the tomb. And behold, there was a great earthquake; for an angel of the Lord descended from heaven, and came and rolled back the stone from the door, and sat on it. His countenance was like lightning, and his clothing as white as snow. And the guards shook for fear of him, and became like dead men. But the angel answered and said to the women, "Do not be afraid, for I know that you seek Jesus who was crucified. He is not here; for He is risen, as He said. Come, see the place where the Lord lay" (Matthew 28:1-6).

Jesus Christ, who had been crucified and killed just three days before, was no longer dead. How appropriate it is that He was raised up on the day of the firstfruits celebration! As Paul explained, "Now Christ is risen from the dead, and has become the firstfruits of those who have fallen asleep" (1 Corinthians 15:20). Jesus wasn't just raised on the day of the firstfruits, He *is* the firstfruits. Of course, the implication of the word *first* is that there will be more to follow. Paul, speaking of the resurrection of the dead, said, "Each one in his own order: Christ the firstfruits, afterward those who are Christ's at His coming" (verse 23). In the same way that Christ was brought back from the dead to experience eternal life, we who belong to Him will one day be brought back to a life that will never end.

There is a debate among many as to whether it is appropriate to designate Sunday as the Lord's day. Of course it is! Sunday, as the first day of the week, is the day of firstfruits. It is a day of celebration. It is a day for recognizing the wonderful hope that is found in Jesus Christ, who died for our sins and rose again on the first day of the week to give us life everlasting.

THE FEAST OF WEEKS (PENTECOST)

When it comes to God's plans, some people are always preoccupied with counting. How many weeks have passed? How many blood moons have risen in the night sky? They do this in an attempt to crack some alleged code or find some hidden insight into what God has planned. Unfortunately, all this counting does is shift people's attention away from truths the Lord has clearly written in Scripture and toward speculations that aren't in Scripture.

When the Bible wants you to look into a specific event or phenomenon, it tells you to look. And when the Bible wants you to count something, it tells you to count. Leviticus 23 says,

> You shall count for yourselves from the day after the Sabbath, from the day that you brought the sheaf of the wave offering: seven Sabbaths shall be completed. Count fifty days to the day after the seventh Sabbath; then you shall offer a new grain offering to the Lord...And you shall proclaim on the same day that it is a holy convocation to you (verses 15-16,21).

Celebrate the Feast of the Firstfruits, count 50 days, then on that fiftieth day, gather together before the Lord.

Jewish tradition holds that it took 50 days of desert walking for the Jews to make it from Egypt to Mt. Sinai. Once there, according to the Talmud (the book of Jewish rabbinic writings), a bizarre phenomenon occurred when the law was given to Moses on the mountain. As the law was brought to the people of Israel, the sound waves of God's voice became visible and appeared as tongues of fire among the gathered listeners.[3]

Many years later, something similar yet much more powerful occurred:

> When the Day of Pentecost had fully come, they were all with one accord in one place. And suddenly there came a sound from heaven, as of a rushing mighty wind, and it filled the whole house where they were sitting. Then there appeared to them divided tongues, as of fire, and one sat upon each of them. And they were all filled with the Holy Spirit and began to speak with other tongues, as the Spirit gave them utterance (Acts 2:1-4).

The disciples had gathered together in one accord—and, no, this isn't a commercial for Honda. Like all other good Jews on that day, they were celebrating the Feast of Weeks. Remember, the disciples, like Jesus, were righteous, law-following Jews.

By the way, I recently heard a pastor make the claim that Jesus was not a Jew, but a Palestinian. I don't know what Bible he was reading, but it certainly wasn't the right one. Jesus was as Jewish as a Jew could be.

While the Jews were all celebrating the shadow of the coming of the law on that Day of Pentecost (*Pentecost* is the Greek name for the Feast of Weeks, and means "fifty"), God brought about substance that was much more powerful. He sent the Holy Spirit. This was something new; the Jews had never experienced it before. Nor had the world ever seen anything like this.

In the Old Testament, the Holy Spirit's ministry was very different than what we now experience. Back then, He had more of a hit-and-run connection with His recipients. When a certain task needed doing or a certain message needed to be communicated, the Holy Spirit would come upon a specific servant or messenger and enable him or her to do what the Lord was calling that person to do. Once the mission was accomplished, the Holy Spirit would leave that person. At Pentecost, this all changed. This time the Holy Spirit permanently came into that group of early believers. He filled them and sealed them, and the church was born.

This sealing by the Holy Spirit is a wonderful gift from the Lord. First, it ensures that the Spirit is never taken from us. The Holy Spirit is like the ultimate superglue. Once something is sealed by God, it cannot be opened again.

Second, this sealing marks us as belonging to the Lord. In the past, when a letter was being sent from one important person to another, the missive would be sealed with clay or wax. A glob of the substance would be placed upon the closure, and a seal would be impressed upon it, leaving a mark of ownership. Similarly, God has given us the Holy Spirit as a seal of ownership. When He sees us, He knows that we belong to Him because He sees His seal upon our hearts. We are His, and no one can take us away from Him.

There is one more shadow that is played out in the Feast of Weeks, and it has to do with the primary actors in the wave ritual—the priests. Why was this honor given to the tribe of Levi? They were not the firstborn. They were not the largest. Levi himself was a violent man, who, along with his brother Simeon, wiped out a whole town in retribution for the rape of their sister, Dinah.

The story of Levi's choosing begins at Mount Sinai. Moses had been up on the mountain for weeks without sending word to the people below about how things were going. In fact, there hadn't even been a sighting of him. People naturally started to wonder if something had happened to the old man. Then someone remembered that Moses had gone up without any food or water (and there had been no indication of Domino's or Jimmy John's running some provisions up the hill). There's no way Moses could still be alive, they assumed. It was much more likely that God had gotten frustrated with Moses, and their fearless leader had been fried by a lightning bolt or buried under an inconvenient landslide.

With no visible leader and with an invisible God who was getting a little too uncomfortable to be around, the people began to get restless. They wanted a new leader—a guy they could boss around a little and who wasn't so grumpy all the time. They also wanted a kinder, gentler god—a god they could see, touch, and wheel around on a little cart. They found the malleable leader in Moses' brother, Aaron, and they discovered the happy little god in a fire.

"Make us a god," they said. And Aaron replied, "Uh…okay." The people brought Aaron their gold earrings, and, as he later unconvincingly told Moses, "I cast [the gold] into the fire, and this calf came out" (Exodus 32:24). Apparently, those hours he spent molding and shaping the baby-cow god had slipped his mind.

Of course, up on the mountain, God knew exactly what was happening down below, and He clued Moses in. One speedy journey down the mountain and a couple broken tablets later, Moses lowered the boom. The people were out of control in their depraved and lustful worship of this idol, so, as we saw a few chapters back,

> Moses stood in the entrance of the camp, and said, "Whoever is on the LORD's side—come to me!" And all the sons of Levi gathered themselves together to him. And he said to them, "Thus says the LORD God of Israel: 'Let every man put his sword on his side, and go in and out from entrance to entrance throughout the camp,

> and let every man kill his brother, every man his com-
> panion, and every man his neighbor.'" So the sons of
> Levi did according to the word of Moses. And about
> three thousand men of the people fell that day (Exodus
> 32:26-28).

Because of the faithfulness of this one tribe in their zeal to protect the holiness and righteousness of the Lord, He set them apart to be His special servants.

A couple millennia later, the substance of Pentecost is played out once again—this time, among those disciples and followers of Jesus who were waiting and praying. Jesus was gone, but He had told them to wait. The Father had something special for them, and they would know it when they saw it. Suddenly, the stillness was broken by a sound like a huge gust of wind. Tongues of fire appeared and descended upon each person, and with those flames came the promised Holy Spirit, filling each one to the full.

With the Holy Spirit came a power, a boldness, and a strange new ability to speak languages they had never learned. Bursting out of their room with the same zeal and confidence with which the Levites had rushed through the camp, these newly anointed evangelists poured out into the streets, which were crowded with Feast of Weeks visitors from all over the Roman Empire. These travelers, so used to trying to communicate through an Aramaic language barrier, suddenly heard the gospel of Jesus Christ in their own language. A revival was taking place—a true harvest of souls! Luke tells us, "Those who gladly received his word were baptized; and that day about three thousand souls were added to them" (Acts 2:41). Three thousand people received eternal life in one day.

If the number 3,000 sounds strangely familiar, one only needs to look back to the story of the golden calf. Three thousand were slaughtered for their rebellion. The law was sufficient for revealing sin, and Christ's sacrifice was sufficient for removing sin. The law kills, but the Spirit gives life.

THE FEAST OF TRUMPETS

After a long period of no feasts, transitioning from the spring celebrations to the fall, we come to the Feast of Trumpets. This ranks number one on the Most Bizarre Holiday on the Jewish Calendar list. "Hey, everybody, come to Jerusalem. We'll blow the trumpets, then you can go back home."

The shadow is spelled out in three short verses:

> The LORD spoke to Moses, saying, "Speak to the children of Israel, saying: 'In the seventh month, on the first day of the month, you shall have a sabbath-rest, a memorial of blowing of trumpets, a holy convocation. You shall do no customary work on it; and you shall offer an offering made by fire to the LORD'" (Leviticus 23:23-25).

When we think of a trumpet blowing in Israel, it's easy to mentally default to the shofar. Even today, you can go to the Western Wall and see young men, at their Bar Mitzvah, being lifted up in the air to the echoing blast of one of these hollowed-out rams' horns.

The feast trumpets, however, were different. They are described in Numbers 10:1-10. There were two of them, both hammered out of silver. What was to be the purpose of these trumpets outside of the feast days? They were all about getting ready—get ready to move, get ready to fight, get ready for something or someone special to come.

Why not use the shofar, a sound that the people would be used to? Why silver? Silver is a precious metal, but not too precious. It's not gold. While special, these trumpets were meant to be utilitarian. They were not just for show.

Why two? To answer this, we need to look at one of Jesus' parables, and here is where we will find the substance. When Jesus was giving the Olivet Discourse, you'll recall that He was sitting on the Mount of Olives having a private conversation with His disciples and talking about the signs of the end times. He said, "Now learn this parable from the fig tree: When its branch has already become tender and puts forth leaves, you know that summer is near. So you also, when you see all these things, know that it is near—at the doors!" (Matthew 24:32-33). What is important, He points out, is not the fig tree that was standing nearby, but the parable about the fig tree. Remember, the fig tree represents something else.

When we look back to the prophet Joel, we read, "A nation has come up against My land, strong, and without number; his teeth are the teeth of a lion, and he has the fangs of a fierce lion. He has laid waste My vine, and ruined My fig tree" (Joel 1:6-7). Who is the land this nation has just laid waste to? It is God's land—the nation of Israel, which is God's fig tree. This is confirmed by the prophet Hosea: "I found Israel like grapes in the wilderness; I saw your fathers as the firstfruits on the fig tree in its first season" (Hosea 9:10). The patriarchs of Israel were the firstfruits produced by God's fig tree—His holy nation.

So when God spoke through the prophet Ezekiel about the return of His people to the land, saying, "I will take you from among the nations, gather you out of all countries, and bring you into your own land" (Ezekiel 36:24), He was talking about the harvest of the fig tree. The ruined tree of Joel 1:7 will be restored, and when it becomes fruitful again, God will gather His people back to their own land.

The same pastor who said that Jesus was a Palestinian also spoke about the land of Israel. He said that the Jews were interlopers, that they had driven out the rightful owners of the land. And who does he say were the rightful owners? The Palestinians, of course. What would this pastor say to Abraham, who had first been given the land by God? What would he say to the prophet Ezekiel, through whom the Lord promised a Jewish return to their land? The Bible makes it clear that the land belongs to God, and He can give it to whomever He chooses. The nation He has chosen to give the land to is Israel.

God made it clear that He would be the One gathering His people from the nations, and that He would be the One bringing them back to the land. I was not the one who brought my grandparents to Israel from the Holocaust. God allowed them to survive. God brought them all the way back to Israel. No one else helped them. No country came alongside when Israel struggled to become a nation and maintain its existence. God and God alone made it happen.

Back to our original substance question: Why two trumpets? Israel, God's fig tree, is the fulfillment of one of the trumpets. Remember, a trumpet announces that someone is coming or that something is happening. Isaiah wrote, "'You are My witnesses,' says the LORD, 'And My servant whom I have chosen, that you may know and believe Me, and understand that I am He. Before Me there was no God formed, nor shall there be after Me'" (Isaiah 43:10). God's working in the nation of Israel, particularly the way He has brought the people back to the land, is a witness of His power and His plan. Do you wonder if there truly is an all-powerful God? Then look at the Jews, who were once scattered all over the world, and who are now back in a thriving nation, just as the Lord had promised. This is why the enemy wants to destroy Israel. He is always seeking ways to destroy the evidence and kill the witness.

The second trumpet is revealed by Jesus. As He is about to return to heaven, He says to His disciples, "You shall receive power when the Holy Spirit has come upon you; and you shall be witnesses to Me in Jerusalem, and in all Judea and Samaria, and to the end of the earth" (Acts 1:8). Israel is the first witness of God's power, and the church is the second. Together we are the only true witnesses of God in this world, and that is why we will always end up suffering together. Anyone who is against Israel is typically anti-Christian as well.

But there is more substance to this blasting of the trumpets. Paul wrote of the time that God is going to remove His church from the earth: "Behold, I tell you a mystery: We shall not all sleep, but we shall all be changed—in a moment, in the twinkling of an eye, at the last trumpet. For the trumpet will sound, and the dead will be raised incorruptible, and we shall be changed" (1 Corinthians 15:51-52). Jesus is coming for His bride, and the announcement of His return will be made with the blast of a trumpet.

Since the reformation of Israel into a nation in 1948, the two witnesses have once again been blasting the warning. The existence of Israel and the testimony of the church are saying to all who will listen, "Get ready—someone is coming, and something is about to happen." The someone is Jesus, and the something happening is the Lord rapturing His church—"in a moment, in the twinkling of an eye, at the last trumpet."

I believe that in this substance of the Lord's return, the Feast of Trumpets is not a single event. There have been a series of trumpet blasts—events that have been predicted by the prophets of the Old Testament—and there will be more to come. One day there will come the sound of a trumpet. In that moment, we who belong to Christ will be out of here—taken up into the presence of our Savior.

There is one more resounding of the trumpets, which will introduce our final substance. On the Mount of Olives, Jesus said to His disciples,

> The sign of the Son of Man will appear in heaven, and then all the tribes of the earth will mourn, and they will see the Son of Man coming on the clouds of heaven with power and great glory. And He will send His angels with a great sound of a trumpet, and they will gather together His elect from the four winds, from one end of heaven to the other (Matthew 24:30-31).

When Jesus Christ returns to the very place that He spoke those words, He will be preceded by the trumpets announcing His arrival. This fanfare is different from that of the rapture. The rapture trumpets that are heard in heaven will announce His departure to gather His people. The trumpets at the second coming that are heard here on earth will announce His arrival with His people.

There is one more difference between the rapture trumpets and those of the second coming. We don't know when the rapture ones will sound. Nobody knows—"not even the angels in heaven, nor the Son" (Mark 13:32). However, with the second coming, we know exactly when it will happen. Every other feast has an exact date for its fulfillment. The feast of trumpets is no different. The substance of Passover was fulfilled on Passover. The substance of the Day of Atonement will be fulfilled on the Day of Atonement. In the same way, the Feast of Trumpets will find its fulfillment during the Feast of Trumpets. When the seven years of the tribulation reach their end, all should look to the sky at the time of this great feast. If they do, they will see the King of kings and Lord of lords descending to the Mount of Olives to take His rightful seat on His throne in Jerusalem.

THE DAY OF ATONEMENT

This is the sixth of the annual gatherings, and the most tragic. The Lord said to Moses, "The tenth day of this seventh month shall be the Day of Atonement. It shall be a holy convocation for you; you shall afflict your souls, and offer an offering made by fire to the LORD" (Leviticus 23:27). "Afflict your souls" means being aware that we are utterly helpless. There is nothing that we can do to save ourselves. The Jews take "afflict" to mean fasting. However, when the Bible wants us to fast, it tells us to fast, and there is no fasting mentioned here. This is a day of recognizing mankind's total inadequacy and God's total sufficiency.

The substance of the Day of Atonement is found in the words of the prophet Zechariah: "I will pour on the house of David and on the inhabitants of Jerusalem the Spirit of grace and supplication; then they will look on Me whom they pierced. Yes, they will mourn for Him as one mourns for his only son, and grieve for Him as one grieves for a firstborn" (Zechariah 12:10). When the Jewish people see Jesus returning on His white horse, His feet standing on the Mount of Olives, and the church surrounding Him as we return with Him, the remnant of Israel will finally recognize Him for who He is. They will mourn for Him as they look on the One whom their ancestors pierced.

That mourning, however, will turn into wonderful joy. This revelation of the Messiah will lead to the blessed promise that we read of in Romans 11. A revival will come among the chosen people of God, and it will be so powerful and so far-reaching that "all Israel will be saved" (verse 26). Leave it to God to take a shadow that is so focused on sorrow and mourning, and turn it into a reality so filled with grace and rejoicing.

THE FEAST OF TABERNACLES

The final feast on the Jewish calendar is the Feast of Tabernacles. "Speak to the children of Israel, saying: 'The fifteenth day of this seventh month shall be the Feast of Tabernacles for seven days to the LORD'" (Leviticus 23:34). Unlike the Day of Atonement, which is the shortest and the most sorrowful of the festivals, the Feast of Tabernacles is the longest and the happiest.

This week-long celebration was unique amongst the feasts in that it was a time for all people in Israel—Jews and Gentiles alike—to come to Jerusalem to celebrate:

> Gather the people together, men and women and little ones, and the stranger who is within your gates, that they may hear and that they may learn to fear the LORD your God and carefully observe all the words of this law, and that their children, who have not known it, may hear and learn to fear the LORD your God as long as you live in the land which you cross the Jordan to possess (Deuteronomy 31:12-13).

As the people gathered and crowded the streets of Jerusalem, they set up small temporary shelters—booths or tabernacles—to stay in. The purpose of the feast was to present the annual reading of God's law. The reason for the booths was to remind the people of how they once had to live in temporary housing for 40 years as they waited to enter into the Promised Land.

The substance of this feast is found in the words of the prophet Zechariah. He tells us that we will continue to celebrate this feast for a very long time to come. However, in that future time, we will celebrate in the presence of the Lord Himself: "It shall come to pass that everyone who is left of all the nations which came against Jerusalem shall go up from year to year to worship the King, the LORD of hosts, and to keep the Feast of Tabernacles" (Zechariah 14:16). As before, this future feast will be for all people. All will go to tabernacle before the Lord, and He will be there to tabernacle with His people.

ARE THE FESTIVALS FULFILLED?

Each of the festivals on the Jewish calendar have a deeper and more powerful meaning. Four have already been fulfilled, one is being carried out now, and two are yet to come. Passover was fulfilled in the crucifixion of Christ, Unleavened Bread was lived out in the sinless life of our Lord, Firstfruits was celebrated in His glorious resurrection, and Weeks saw the pouring out of the Holy Spirit on the church.

Today, we have Trumpets blowing around us as world events draw us closer and closer to the return of Christ. The Day of Atonement will have a wonderful fulfillment when all Israel comes to Christ, and they and the church will Tabernacle together in the millennial kingdom with God Himself.

When will the final trumpet sound, finishing the Feast of Trumpets and opening the door for the final two feasts? We don't know. If God wanted us to know the exact date, He would have set up a group meeting on Google Calendar. We do know that the day approaches ever closer with each trumpet blast.

> Let's make sure our words and actions put forth a clear message that Jesus is coming soon, and that all need to be ready to meet Him.

As we wait, we need to ask ourselves: What kind of trumpet are we? Again, trumpets are used as warnings and signals that someone is coming and something is about to happen. Our lives must be sounding the clear warning blasts that let people know they need to be prepared. Paul warned, "If the trumpet makes an uncertain sound, who will prepare for battle?" (1 Corinthians 14:8). Let's make sure our words and actions put forth a clear message that Jesus is coming soon, and that all need to be ready to meet Him.

CHAPTER 7

THE VIEW FROM THE MIDDLE EAST

IF YOU HAD TO STOP AT A RAILROAD crossing in Bowling Green, Ohio, on May 15, 2001, it's quite possible that your delay might have been caused by a 47-car CSX train rolling past. By every indication, this train may have seemed to be like every other train in your lifetime for which you've waited, fingers impatiently tapping on your steering wheel as it goes by. However, if you had looked closely, you would have noticed one frightening difference about this train—the engine compartment was completely empty. Due to an operator error at a rail yard just outside of Toledo, the engine began rolling on its own. Soon it was cruising south at 51 miles per hour, taking the attached 47 train cars along for an engineer-less joyride.

Panic set in fairly quickly. Not only was there the fear of a possible derailment in a populated area, there was the additional danger of the presence of two tank cars filled with phenol. This toxic liquid could cause a lot of severe problems if touched or inhaled. Derailers were put on the track in an unpopulated area to try to force the train off the tracks, but the runaway engine plowed right over them. The police tried shooting an emergency fuel cutoff switch, but that also was to no avail.

Desperate, a new plan was devised. Two engineers took an engine and drove it to a secondary track alongside the out-of-control train's path. After the train roared past, they pulled out behind it. Carefully, they accelerated until they were just behind the final car. Easing ever closer, they finally heard the clack of their engine locking onto the last car. They immediately applied their dynamic brakes and prayed. Mile by mile slid by as their engine strained to counter the pull of the driver-less engine up front. Finally, when their speed reached 11 miles an hour, a train master was able to run alongside the train, pull himself up, and shut down the engine.[1]

There are many people who see the Middle East as being like that out-of-control train. War in Syria. Nuclear ambitions in Iran. ISIS slaughtering people indiscriminately. The Middle East is hurtling ever forward, and there doesn't seem to be a driver in sight. Who is going to step in to slow things down? Will Russia? Or the United States? Or maybe Israel or Turkey or Iran? Maybe the question is not who will stop it, but can anyone stop it or even slow it down?

Or maybe we need to take one more step backward. Maybe the question is not, Who will stop the out-of-control Middle East, but rather, Is the Middle East really out of control? Could it be that instead of wild mayhem, what we are witnessing is all part of a larger plan? Is it possible that even though we don't see an engineer in the driver's seat, there is still someone there steering this train?

The answer is yes. Not only is it possible, but that is exactly what's happening. The runaway train of the Middle East has not run away at all. It is 100 percent on course, locked into a rail line that was laid out for it many centuries ago.

EXPECT THE UNEXPECTED

One of the greatest mistakes we can make when it comes to understanding God is to assume that He will act how we think He should act. Since it makes sense to us, then it should certainly make sense to Him. Good people should have easy, happy lives. Bad people should have nasty, uncomfortable lives until they learn to straighten up into good people. When God is involved, everything should run smoothly, and peace will abound. When God removes His hand, then everything will speed toward destruction.

But is that really the way God works?

Reading through the Bible, we find out quickly that God works very differently than we would expect. Often it is because we are filtering what we see through our own limited perspective. In the Psalms we read, "O LORD, how great are Your works! Your thoughts are very deep. A senseless man does not know, nor does a fool understand this. When the wicked spring up like grass, and when all the workers of iniquity flourish, it is that they may be destroyed forever" (Psalm 92:5-7). The writer of this psalm was looking around and trying to figure out why it appeared as if the wicked were doing so well. Everything they touched seemed to turn to gold, while those who followed God seemed to be struggling just to get by.

This was the struggle that almost cost David's chief musician, Asaph, his faith. He wrote, "As for me, my feet had almost stumbled; my steps had nearly slipped. For I was envious of the boastful, when I saw the prosperity of the wicked" (Psalm 73:2-3). There is a quote frequently attributed to Groucho Marx that goes, "Who you gonna believe, me or your lying eyes?" God could ask us that same question.

Our lying eyes only give us the temporary view. We can't see the future, we know only a little of the past, and even in the present our view is limited to what is directly around us. We may think the wicked are doing great while the righteous suffer, but that is only because we can't see the world through God's eyes. He has the eternal view. He not only knows that evil will be destroyed forever, He also has the perfect plan for making that happen. While our eyes and minds can only comprehend checkers, God is playing a game of 3-D chess.

THE JEWS? REALLY?

This earth that we live on belongs to God. He made it, and He will carry out His plans for it. King David wrote, "The earth is the LORD's, and all its fullness, the world and those who dwell therein. For He has founded it upon the seas, and established it upon the waters" (Psalm 24:1-2). Did you know that the Hebrew word translated "create," *bara*, is only used with God as its subject? In other words, only God can create something out of nothing. Humans can be creative—they can take the materials that God has already made and fashion them into something that looks, feels, smells, and tastes different. However, only God can start with just a thought and bring that thought into reality.

> Everything God does is right. All His ways are perfect. This is what gives us peace when the world seems out of control.

Because God is the Creator of all things, everything falls under His right of ownership. He made it all, and it all belongs to Him. Therefore, He can do whatever He likes with it. That would be a terrifying proposition if God were different than what we know Him to be. One only needs to look at the long line of sadistic Roman emperors to see what happens when unlimited power and authority reside in unworthy hands. Our Creator, however, is worthy. He is holy and righteous. Everything He does is right. All His ways are perfect. This is what gives us peace when the world seems out of control. God is in the driver's seat, and He is working out His perfect plan.

One example of God carrying out His perfect plan that still has many people scratching their heads is when He selected Israel to be His chosen people. The Jews? Really? Why didn't He choose the Chinese? There are so many more of them. Or what about the Swiss? They like to get along with everybody, and their chocolate is delicious. Again, God's logic is very different than ours.

It all started when the Lord created Adam and Eve. Everything was going so well, and the world could still bear that God-perfect label of "Good." But then came the tree, the fruit, and the sin. By the time Genesis 6 rolls around, God is sorry that He created humanity. He's ready to scrap the whole lot. Yet there's one guy—Noah—who is still doing it right. God rescues Noah and his family, and from this man's lineage He puts His eye on a pagan man living out in Mesopotamia. This pagan man is the father of the Jews—Abram, who later became Abraham.

What did the Lord see in Abram? Truly, only God Himself knows. He says to him,

> Get out of your country,
> from your family
> and from your father's house,
> to a land that I will show you.
> I will make you a great nation;
> I will bless you
> and make your name great;

and you shall be a blessing.
I will bless those who bless you,
and I will curse him who curses you;
and in you all the families of the earth shall be blessed
(Genesis 12:1-3).

Have you ever wondered why the Jews have been persecuted so severely over the centuries? Look no further than this promise of God to Abram. God chose this people to be the ones through whom He would introduce Himself to the rest of the world. Through them He would make His Word and His plan known. Through them He would make His love, grace, mercy, holiness, justice, power, wisdom, and patience known. Through the Jews, the world would learn of God's desire for relationship with His creation. Through this nation would come the One who would make that God-to-man relationship possible.

Jesus was a Jew, born of the tribe of Judah, just as I am. When Jesus was born from this Abrahamic line of people, He emerged proclaiming loudly who God truly is. While the nation of Israel announced God with a whisper, Jesus proclaimed His Father with a bullhorn. His whole life declared the glory of God. He went so far as to boldly claim, "I and My Father are one" (John 10:30). In other words, there is no difference between what you see in Jesus and what you see in God the Father.

Yet even the disciples didn't get it. The night before Jesus was crucified, He told His inner circle, "If you had known Me, you would have known My Father also; and from now on you know Him and have seen Him" (John 14:7). But Philip, after spending three years listening to Jesus' sermons, watching all His healings, and engaging Him in private conversations over the many miles they walked together, still asked Jesus to show them the Father. Astounded at this lack of understanding, Jesus said, "Have I been with you so long, and yet you have not known Me, Philip? He who has seen Me has seen the Father; so how can you say, 'Show us the Father'? Do you not believe that I am in the Father, and the Father in Me?" (verses 9-10). This is the equivalent of Jesus knocking on the disciples' heads and saying, "Hello? Is anybody in there? Are you guys listening to Me at all?"

Once Jesus came and showed perfectly who the Father is, the time arrived for a response from humanity: Here's God. Now, what are you going to do about it? When Paul visited Athens, he was invited to speak before all the great thinkers of the Areopagus. Challenging them with the futility of their ambiguous polytheism, he called them to face and respond to the reality of the one true God. "Since we are the offspring of God, we ought not to think that the Divine Nature is like gold or silver or stone, something shaped by art and man's devising. Truly, these times of ignorance God overlooked, but now commands all men everywhere to repent" (Acts 17:29-30). We cannot plead ignorance now that the Truth has visited the earth.

This same imperative to repent can be blanketed across today's world, and much of today's church. There is no salvation without repentance. To repent is to recognize one's wrongdoing and make a deep-hearted commitment to turn from it. We should not settle for watered-down churches that preach ear candy in an attempt to keep the seats filled, the parishioners happy, and the offering plates full. God has appointed a day when He will judge the world. Enough game-playing. Jesus came, and now it's time to take our lives and our mission seriously.

THE LAND OF ISRAEL? REALLY?

Not only did God choose one people, He also chose one region of the world. And the arid, dusty Middle East today seems just as unlikely a location for God's plan to show Himself to the world as the

Jews were unlikely a people. However, what we see today is not how things were. Back in the days of the Old Testament, the area known as the Fertile Crescent was highly prized and regularly fought over.

The word *crescent* speaks of the shape of the region, which looks like a downward-pointing French croissant on the top of the Arabian Desert. Following a path north and west, this area starts in what is now modern-day Iran and eastern Iraq, crosses over to Turkey, then back down western Syria, Lebanon, and Israel. The label *fertile* is due to the land's agricultural and technological productiveness. As a result of the plentiful resources of the region, many of the great early civilizations were born here—the Akkadians, Sumerians, Assyrians, Babylonians, Medes, and Persians. Each empire was a superpower of its time, and if these superpowers wanted to trade with the other great long-lasting superpower, Egypt, there was only one route for doing so, and it passed right through the promised inheritance of Abraham and his descendants—the land of Israel.

There was no more strategic place for God to announce His existence to the world than that little strip of land by the Mediterranean. After God snatched His people from Pharaoh's bondage down in Egypt, this land of milk and honey is where He directed Moses to lead them. They were the means God used to show His power and faithfulness to the world. They were also the means God used to test the surrounding nations.

Around 20 years ago, I began traveling the world. My first speaking trip was to the Philippines, and I remember being excited and terrified at the same time. A lot of prayer and preparation preceded getting on the plane from Tel Aviv. One of the insights the Lord gave to me as I prayed was that I would be able to tell whether a church I spoke at was a truth-telling church on the basis of what it taught about Israel. A church's view of God's chosen people can serve as a litmus test for truth. If a church disregarded Israel and relegated the nation to the dustbin of history, then most likely I couldn't trust it to be a truth-telling church. If it dishonored the people whom God had honored with His name and His Messiah, then I found it hard to believe that the Lord would honor that church. Remember God's promise to Abraham: "I will bless those who bless you, and I will curse him who curses you" (Genesis 12:3). In the same way that God watches how nations and people treat Israel, I watch how churches treat the chosen people.

Unfortunately, Israel turned out to be a poor mouthpiece for God and the people set a very low standard for faithfulness. In fact, not only was Israel a test to the nations, but the nations were a test to Israel to see whether the people would follow God. After Joshua failed to lead the Israelites to a complete clearing out of the Promised Land, the Lord decided to leave the remaining pagan population, saying, "I also will no longer drive out before them any of the nations which Joshua left when he died, so that through them I may test Israel, whether they will keep the ways of the LORD, to walk in them as their fathers kept them, or not" (Judges 2:21-22). Would Israel succumb to the temptation to follow pagan gods like all the other nations? The answer is an emphatic *yes.*

Time after time, the people of Israel left the one living God to run after imitation gods made of gold and silver and wood. And every time they did, a divinely orchestrated smackdown would come their way in the form of an invading army and subsequent subjugation. As this cycle of rebellion was repeated, the power and will of the Almighty God were shown in all their splendor.

In Jeremiah 25, God called up a great army to go forth and cause some major destruction. Who was at the head of this army? A great king of Judah? A man descended from the line of David? That would be impossible, because it was against the nation of Judah that this army was being sent.

Thus says the LORD of hosts: "Because you have not heard My words, behold, I will send and take all the families of the north," says the LORD, "and Nebuchadnezzar the king of Babylon, My servant, and will bring them against this land, against its inhabitants, and against these nations all around, and will utterly destroy them, and make them an astonishment, a hissing, and perpetual desolations" (Jeremiah 25:8-9).

God punished the unfaithfulness of His people using a pagan king of a pagan empire—Nebuchadnezzar, whom God calls "My servant."

Does this mean Nebuchadnezzar was doing good by bringing death and destruction against this helpless nation? Absolutely not. Three verses later in Jeremiah 25, God said, "Then it will come to pass, when seventy years are completed, that I will punish the king of Babylon and that nation, the land of the Chaldeans, for their iniquity...and I will make it a perpetual desolation" (Jeremiah 25:12). "How is that fair?" some may cry out. "Doesn't that mean God was punishing them for doing His will?"

No, God punished them for their sin. The will to attack was their own. The desire for violence and destruction came from their own tainted hearts. God, in His infinite power, was able to use the sin that the Babylonians were going to commit anyway to accomplish His will.

> Even when people are doing all they can to rebel against the righteous ways of God, He is still in control.

When Joseph's father, Jacob, died in Egypt, all his brothers were terrified that he would finally execute revenge against them for selling him into slavery. But Joseph's response was, "Do not be afraid, for am I in the place of God? But as for you, you meant evil against me; but God meant it for good, in order to bring it about as it is this day, to save many people alive" (Genesis 50:19-20). Even when people are doing all they can to rebel against the righteous ways of God, He is still in control.

MUSLIM VS. MUSLIM

Throughout history, the Middle East has been a hot spot for violence and war. But, as we've seen, even when it may appear that the region is in constant upheaval, God is still in control. Today, much of what is happening centers on the conflict between the two big Middle Eastern empires, Saudi Arabia and Iran. Many people are surprised by the fact that these two powerful Muslim nations, both of which have a history of terrorism against the West, are such mortal enemies of each other. Their conflict is not over disputed territory or natural resources. Instead, it's over religious factions within Islam. Saudi Arabia, along with 87 to 90 percent of all Muslims,[2] is Sunni, while Iran is Shiite. What seems like a simple difference in terms to those in the West can get you killed in the Middle East.

When Muhammad died in AD 632, there was disagreement over who should take over the reins of Islam. One group believed that a trusted aide of Muhammad, Abu Bakr, should become the new caliph (leader). In their eyes, the position should go to the best man for the job, determined by a consensus of the leadership. This branch of Islam is called Sunni after the phrase *Ahl al-Sunnah*, which means "People of the Tradition."

Another group believed that Muhammad had designated his cousin and son-in-law, Ali, to be the next great leader and that all leaders moving forward should come from Ali's line. These are the Shiites, after the phrase *Shiat Ali*, which means "Party of Ali."

Through the centuries, this dispute over leadership succession has led to innumerable acts of violence and countless lives being lost. Believe it or not, Iran and Saudi Arabia hate each other more than they hate Israel.

Currently, Shiite Iran is sending arms all around the Middle East to stoke the fires of sectarianism. They are arming governments or rebels in Lebanon, Syria, Yemen, and Iraq. To counter these measures, Sunni Saudi Arabia is using their own tactics. In March 2018, following a friendly match between the Saudi and Iraqi football teams, King Salman of Saudi Arabia, in a move that would have made Dale Carnegie proud, offered to build Iraq a 135,000-seat stadium.[3] "Here's a giant stadium—let's be friends. Now, how about we gang up on those nasty Iranians?"

Not all Saudi tactics have been this congenial, however. In November 2017, Lebanese prime minister Saad Hariri flew to Saudi Arabia. Once the Saudis had him in the country, they made the decision to extend his stay indefinitely until he denounced Iran and resigned as prime minister.[4]

With the bad blood getting worse and the fear of a nuclear Iran becoming more real, it is very possible that current tensions could turn into an all-out war. There are political, economic, and religious upheavals all across the Middle East, and meanwhile, Israel sits at the center of it all, enjoying a time of unprecedented prosperity and security.

PSALM 83 TO EZEKIEL 38

Everything that we see taking place in the Middle East has been talked about in the Bible. It is not random. It is not out of control. What we are observing is a transition like we have never seen before. I believe that as we watch the events in the world around us we are witnessing the shift from the reality of Psalm 83 to the eve of Ezekiel 38. The psalmist Asaph penned these prophetic words:

Do not keep silent, O God!
Do not hold Your peace,
and do not be still, O God!
For behold, Your enemies make a tumult;
and those who hate You have lifted up their head.
They have taken crafty counsel against Your people,
and consulted together against Your sheltered ones.
They have said, "Come, and let us cut them off from
being a nation,
that the name of Israel may be remembered no more"
(Psalm 83:1-4).

This frightening prediction tells of an all-out attack on Israel by the surrounding nations. Their goal is genocide—the destruction of the people of Israel to the point that their very name will be remembered no more. This wiping out of God's people was nearly accomplished by Rome in both AD 70 and 135. As we saw in an earlier chapter, Emperor Hadrian, in order to ensure the final destruction of these rebellious people, seemed to take a play right out of the Psalm 83 handbook. Seeking to steal away Israel's national identity, the Roman sovereign renamed Jerusalem *Aelia Capitolina* and Judea *Syria Palestina*. Yet rather than the weight of the Roman Empire crushing the Jews, God's people shot out of Judea like water from a wet sponge. They spread throughout the civilized nations—sometimes assimilating into their new cultures, sometimes creating their own enclaves.

The name *Israel* stayed underground for centuries until 1948, when it suddenly popped back up again. Psalm 83 had not been accomplished by Rome. Israel again existed as a national entity. And as soon as the Jewish nation came back to life, all the surrounding Arab nations did their best to take away that life. Lebanon, Syria, Jordan, Egypt, and Iraq all attacked. God is One who remembers

His covenants, even if they are millennia old. The promises of the Abrahamic covenant kicked into gear, and God put to shame all those who came against Israel.

There is no reason that my fledgling country, with its tiny military, should have been able to withstand the Arab onslaught. We had two planes in our Air Force. With one hand, the pilot would steer with the stick, and with his other hand, he would throw out the bombs. We had a total of five armored vehicles, and most of our army was made up of Holocaust survivors who had never held a weapon in their lives. Yet they devastated the well-equipped and well-trained Arab countries who came up against them. How? It was God. This was true in 1948, and again in 1967.

Numerous times in both wars, Arab platoons fled from what they were sure was a massive Israeli attack. All the sights and sounds around them indicated that they were about to be overrun. Later, it was discovered that there were no Israeli soldiers in those areas at the time. God, in a very real way, sent His heavenly armies to fight for His people.

In another situation, a platoon of Israeli soldiers found themselves in the middle of a minefield. One wrong move could cost the lives of many soldiers. What made the matter worse was that daybreak was not far away. Once the sun came up, they would be exposed and become sitting ducks to the Arab armies. Together, these soldiers prayed for God to intervene. Suddenly, a wind began to blow. It grew in intensity so that the troops had to duck down and cover their eyes and ears from the swirling sand and dirt. This wind blew for 20 minutes. Then, as suddenly as it began, it stopped. Rising up from the ground, the platoon looked around to discover that all of the buried mines had been exposed. The soldiers walked out safely just before the sun rose.

It was not the power of the Israeli army that brought victory. It was God who put the nations to shame. Not only did Israel not lose in 1948, but the nation came out of the war with 30 percent more land than when it entered the conflict. God is in absolute control in the Middle East, carrying out His plans and fulfilling His promises. He has brought the Jews out of the period of Psalm 83. The day of Ezekiel 38 is fast approaching. This is even more evident as we go from the Middle East as a whole and zoom in on Israel in particular.

CHAPTER 8

THE VIEW FROM ISRAEL

WHERE IS GOD IN ISRAEL? That's a question I often get asked, particularly by those who want to write off the modern nation as no different than any other country. It seems that these days, the only God that is evident as you wander around Jerusalem is the Old Testament Jehovah of Judaism, the angry Allah of Islam, or the old-school Adonai of Orthodoxy. Sure, if you look hard enough, you'll find evangelical Christian churches scattered here and there. But they are few and far between.

Of greater concern, however, is the general lack of attention to God on the national scene. In many ways, Israel appears to be a secular state with a thin coat of religiosity—an atheist in rabbi's clothing. One evening of experiencing the nightlife of Tel Aviv will leave visitors confused as to whether they really are in Israel or they've been transported to Amsterdam or San Francisco or Sodom. Zionism's roots are found in the collectivism of Karl Marx, yet it has grown into the capitalistic individualism of Ayn Rand. Again, people ask, where is God in Israel?

A LOOK AT ISRAEL TODAY

The best way to answer this question is to look at the condition of the country today. Over the past ten years, there has been a remarkable change—the Psalm 83 transformation that we learned about in the last chapter. This little nation pressed up against the eastern Mediterranean shore has become a world financial and military power.

First, Israel has become a superpower in the Information Revolution. We are leaders in cybersecurity and other areas of technology and microprocessing. Most people know of the Silicon Valley, located south of San Francisco in California. This region has been on the leading edge of information technology, boasting 39 of the Fortune 100 companies and a seemingly endless supply of start-up ventures.[1] Israel has what is now considered the second Silicon Valley. Dubbed the Silicon Wadi,[2] the area around Tel Aviv boasts more start-up companies per capita than anywhere else in the world.

Financial technology, medical breakthroughs, and agricultural advancements are also areas in which Israel finds itself among the leaders of the pack. Invention after invention and innovation after innovation have kept Israel on the cutting edge of growth. Back in the 1930s, a Polish immigrant to Israel, Simcha Blass, had a lemon tree in his backyard. He watered that tree every day, and the tree did nothing. He decided to water the tree every week, and still nothing. Angry at the tree, he decided to stop watering it altogether. Leaving the hose there, he flew off to an extended conference in Europe.

After a few weeks, Blass returned to find the lemon tree flourishing. He was shocked and more than a little bit frustrated. What had made the difference? Was this a personal thing between him and the tree? Was this the tree's version of sticking it to the man? As he looked for clues, he discovered that there was a small hole in the hose that was letting out water to the lemon tree drip by drip by drip. This made the soil just moist enough to keep the tree happy. The result was 90 percent less water with 90 percent more lemons. That is how drip irrigation was invented. Agriculture was revolutionized, and Mr. Blass ended up with more shekels than he knew what to do with.[3]

An Israeli cow is the most productive cow in the world. Every moo is computerized. With a bovine brilliance, Israeli agriculturists have developed processes that lead these beasts to keep pumping out milk like they can't wait to get it out of their udders.

When the Jews began resettling the land at the turn of the nineteenth century, everywhere they went, the soil was either dry and dusty or swampy and malarial. Now when you look at the land, you'll see the dark green richness of fertility. This is because for decades, Israel has been a leader in water reclamation. Currently, the nation purifies more than 80 percent of its wastewater and uses it again.[4] I was once taken to a nice farm, and a lady there showed me a round pool. The water in it looked so clear and refreshing. She asked me how deep I thought it was. I said, "Two to three meters?"

"Try nine meters," she replied. "Do you want to try some?"

"Of course," I said as she handed me a glass.

I drank it down and was ready to ask for more when she said, "You just drank our sewage water."

There are few statements that can be uttered in any language that will have the same effect on you as hearing those six words. Seeing my reaction (which I'm sure she was hoping to get), she quickly offered an explanation.

She said, "When I flush the water [five more words that did nothing to ease the panic caused by the first six], it comes all the way down to a pool. In this pool are floating water plants, which begin to clean the water. Then the water goes to a second pool with different water plants. By the time it goes to the third pool, the water is perfectly purified."

In Israel, we will find water wherever we can get it. We've even learned how to extract water from the air. You sneeze? We drink. It's amazing.

All these innovations are causing Israel to flourish like never before. The current GDP per capita is well over $41,000.[5] That's more than Japan's GDP, or France's or Great Britain's. Remember, we are a small country surrounded by nations that are in a perpetual state of war with us.

THE MUSLIM INVASION

Compare the growing success of Israel to the decline of the Western world. Over the last ten years, while we have been experiencing incomparable success, the West has been struggling to cope with Muslim invasions into their nations. Right now, there are 700,000 Muslims in Libya waiting for the opportunity to cross the Mediterranean into Europe.[6] And there are Muslims from other countries as well. Why are they doing this? What is causing them to flee? The persecution inflicted by their own regimes is driving them to leave their homes and all they have. It's not just Christians and Jews who are being oppressed by Muslims and are running away, it's also Muslims who are being oppressed by other Muslims.

As millions of Muslims flee the Middle East for the Western world, they are changing the identities of the countries to which they go. Seeing this phenomenon, our government in Israel took measures to ensure we don't lose our own identity the way the West is losing theirs. On July 18, 2018, the Knesset passed the Jewish nation-state law, which declared, in part, that Israel is the home-land of the Jewish people and that Hebrew is the national language.[7]

"But aren't those things self-evident?," some may argue. Yes, they are…for now. But at the rate of Islamization around the world, who knows what we may look like five, ten, or fifteen years from now? So we passed this legislation, and European leaders quickly expressed deep concern over why we would take what they perceived to be a terribly xenophobic action.[8] They ignore the fact our new law states that the Arabic language has a special status. It may not be the state language, but it is still granted a high honor. Maybe those European leaders ignore that fact because even though their countries have far more Muslims than Israel, they have never granted special status to the Arab language.

Europe so much wants Israel to grant the same type of open-border freedoms that they are giving to the Muslim immigrant pop-ulation in their region. No thank you. In Western Europe, violence and terror have continued to grow at alarming rates. Those who can step back and look rationally are starting to understand the position that Israel is in as the only non-Muslim stronghold between Greece and India. The geopolitical situation of Israel is precarious, and we must vigorously protect what we have.

I'm not saying that all Muslims want war. Most don't. Most want to get along with the rest of the world. They want to live at peace and raise their families and be good people. The problem is that these peace-loving Muslims don't speak up for peace. They don't come out against radicals, who are allowed to maintain their rule. They don't condemn when terrorists are treated as martyrs. Terrorists are not martyrs, they're murderers. The good followers of Islam will con-tinue to be marginalized until they finally have the courage to stand up to the radicals and say, "No more."

THE TRIALS OF THE ARAB WORLD

The Arab world is changing. No longer does it have the same power it once had. Plunging oil prices around the world are taking away the big stick that the Middle East once held. Before, the Arab nations could threaten, with the petrodollar, those who did business with Israel. But the power of the petrodollar has been broken. And not only has the price of oil decreased, but the sources for obtaining oil have increased. By the time this book is published, America will have passed Saudi Arabia as the largest exporter of oil and gas in the world.[9] In other words, Israel's best friend is the biggest global energy resource. What this means is that Japan, China, India, South Korea, the Philippines, Singapore, and so many other nations can finally do business with Israel because the Arab energy threats have been neutralized.

The Arab Spring uprisings were a huge benefit to Israel's peace and safety. This series of rebellions was jump-started by President Barack Obama early in his first term. In a speech that he gave in Cairo, Egypt, on June 4, 2009, he essentially told the people of the Arab world that they should all fight for democracy. He encouraged the youth to express their human rights by speaking their minds and demanding a say in their governments.[10]

That stirred up the people in many Middle Eastern nations, where there was already a growing dissatisfaction with the way the countries were being run. Protests began, violence broke out, and more than one million have died[11] thus far in what has become less of an Arab Spring and more of a Muslim Winter. Countries have been collapsing one after another, and all the while, Israel has been growing stronger. Suddenly the country that was at one time anathema to all has become the country other nations want to deal with. Syria and Saudi Arabia are no longer denouncing Israel over the Palestinian issue because they already have enough problems of their own.

Almost every day, rockets are flying into Saudi Arabia—missiles that are made by Iran. Iran manufactures these weapons, smuggles them through the port city of Hodeidah in Yemen, and places them in the hands of Yemeni rebels who fire them over the border.[12] Saudi Arabia is being attacked regularly across their borders with Yemen and Iraq. This puts the Saudis in a position of looking for the enemies of their enemy Iran so they can make them their friend. Who is Iran's biggest enemy in the Middle East? Israel. Who is now becoming the bestie of Israel? Saudi Arabia.

Israel's position in the Middle East continues to improve. The growing friendships with its neighbors is more evidence of the move from Psalm 83 to Ezekiel 38. In the psalm, they are still being attacked from all sides:

> For they have consulted together with one consent;
> they form a confederacy against You:
> the tents of Edom and the Ishmaelites;
> Moab and the Hagrites;
> Gebal, Ammon, and Amalek;
> Philistia with the inhabitants of Tyre;
> Assyria also has joined with them;
> they have helped the children of Lot (verses 5-8).

Two of those nations stand out. The Hagrites are the Egyptians. Ammon is Jordan. No longer are these two nations the sworn enemies of Israel. They have come to the conclusions that the existence of Israel is a fact and that Israel is powerful. It is not in their best interest to fight the Jewish nation anymore. Add to that the newfound friendship Israel has with Saudi Arabia—a country from which both Egypt and Jordan receive billions of dollars each year—and these two countries have decided that the friend of their friend is now their friend.

ISRAEL'S EXPANDING RELATIONSHIPS

Do you need more evidence that Israel is in a better position than ever before? Over the last five years, we have found billions of cubic meters of natural gas.[13] We became an energy superpower overnight. So many governments are coming to invest with us. They want to make sure that they can get a piece of this enormous pie. Israel is using this newfound wealth strategically, taking the profits and putting them into an investment fund so that we can reward the nations who treat us well. "You're my friend? You voted favorably toward us in the UN? Sure, we would love to pour some money into your country."

And speaking of friendships, at the time of this writing, Israel has a closer relationship with the United States than ever before. The crazy rulers around the world have realized that there is someone in the White House who is even crazier than them. President Donald Trump has made some unexpected yet wonderful moves to confirm the United States' partnership with Israel. The US pulled out of the Iran deal. The US moved its embassy to Jerusalem. The US is working with Russia to protect Israel's northern border. The US has imposed the harshest sanctions ever upon Iran. The US pulled out of the UN Human Rights Council because of its biased stand against Israel. The US recognized Israel's sovereignty over the Golan Heights.

Still not convinced? Israel has a closer-than-ever relationship with India. Today, 46 percent of all of Israel's military exports go to India.[14] In July 2017, India's prime minister Narenda Modi made an official visit to Israel. This was the first time ever for an Indian prime minister to do that. In January 2018, Israel's prime minister Benjamin Netanyahu returned the honor.

Israel now has an energy alliance with Greece and Cyprus. Around the same time that Israel discovered its natural gas fields, Cyprus found its own. Since then, Israel and Cyprus have collaborated on developing a pipeline, and they are now conducting joint military operations. Greece, who has historic connections to the recognized Cyprian government, is supporting this Israel/Cyprus connection wholeheartedly.[15] Turkey, who lays claim to Northern Cyprus, is much less thrilled. The more wealth that comes to Cyprus, the less Turkey is needed. Turkey's president Recep Tayyip Erdogan can barely control his anger as he watches Israeli F-16s fly over what he hoped would become his little island.

More, you ask? Israel has developed a strong connection with the Visegrád Group (V4).[16] This alliance of four nations goes all the way back to the fourteenth century, when Bohemia, Poland, and Hungary met together in the town of Visegrád to make commercial, military, and economic agreements. Since that time, these nations have gone through many different eras and iterations, but they united again in the alliance's current form in 1991. The V4 currently consists of Czech Republic, Slovakia, Hungary, and Poland.

In 2017, Prime Minister Netanyahu visited these countries—the first time an Israeli prime minister has done this since the fall of communism. Relationships are being forged, and there has even been talk of these countries moving their embassies to Jerusalem. The European Union's hatred of Israel has been manifest in resolution after resolution and vote after vote. But the EU has been structured so that even one negative vote keeps a resolution from passing. Israel has now fostered the friendship of four "no" votes.

We can't forget about Africa. Israel is back on that continent. In 2016, Netanyahu became the first Israeli prime minister to travel there in decades. On that trip, he stayed in the east part of the continent and visited Uganda, Kenya, Rwanda, and Ethiopia. Then in

2017, along with many other African leaders,[17] he attended an official lunch honoring the inauguration of Kenya's president Uhuru Kenyatta. In the past, much of Africa didn't want anything to do with Israel because the Muslims were strangling them—threatening them financially and militarily. Now here they are eating at the table with Israel.

Finally, we see evangelical Christianity growing all around the world, with the exception of Europe. Many of these evangelicals strongly support Israel. They vote for leaders who support Israel, donate money to ministries in Israel, and pray consistently for the peace of Israel.

We are at a moment in prophetic history when the nation of Israel must be safe. Recently, a survey was taken asking about this very issue, and 89 percent of Israelis indicated that they feel happy and safe in their country.[18] People ask, "How can you feel safe when it is so unsafe there? People all around you want to hurt you." Trust me, it is way safer in Israel than in so many other parts of the world. Compare Israel to Chicago—there are typically more people killed in two weeks in that one American city than in a whole year in the entire nation of Israel.

Israel is in a time when it is safe, secure, and prosperous, as promised in Psalm 83. In Ezekiel 36, God says, "You, O mountains of Israel, you shall shoot forth your branches and yield your fruit to My people Israel, for they are about to come. For indeed I am for you, and I will turn to you, and you shall be tilled and sown" (verses 8-9). What do we see now? A fruitful land feeding not just itself but other nations of the world.

In Ezekiel 37, as Ezekiel stood before a valley filled with warriors who until moments before had been dry bones, God said, "You shall know that I am the LORD, when I have opened your graves, O My people, and brought you up from your graves. I will put My

Spirit in you, and you shall live, and I will place you in your own land. Then you shall know that I, the LORD, have spoken it and performed it" (verses 13-14). This promise was made to those who survived the Holocaust. We have seen how God has taken the dry bones of those people and brought them to the Promised Land of Israel and renewed their lives again. Psalm 83 has been fulfilled. Ezekiel 36 and 37 are being fulfilled. And now, we find ourselves at the doorstep of Ezekiel 38.

GOD IS IN CONTROL

So, who really controls Israel? Even more so, who really controls the Middle East? The Russians believe they control Syria. The Saudis believe that they control the oil. The Americans believe that they can bring peace to the region. But sometimes there is a wide gulf between belief and reality.

> The kings of the earth set themselves,
>   and the rulers take counsel together,
>   against the LORD and against His Anointed, saying,
> "Let us break Their bonds in pieces
>   and cast away Their cords from us."
> He who sits in the heavens shall laugh;
>   the Lord shall hold them in derision (Psalm 2:2-4).

The rulers of this world boast of their power and their plans, and God just sits back and laughs. The One who controls Israel is the same One who controls the Middle East. And He is also the same One who controls the entire world. God is in control, and He will accomplish His will. When you recognize that one truth, you will know more about the future of the Middle East than the best analyst of the best secret service agency in the world.

Twenty years ago, I preached that Russia and Turkey and Iran would unite and come to power in the Middle East. Nobody bought the tape. No one believed it. Thank goodness I didn't have Facebook then, because the views on that video would have been zero. Now we look around and see that what I said would happen is indeed happening. I'm no prophet; I just believe the prophets. I read the Bible, and that is how I know what will happen. God told us what is to come, and He will accomplish it all for His glory, His majesty, and His name.

> God is in control of the Middle East, and He is in control of Israel. That alone should be enough to bring peace to our hearts.

I don't know why so many Christians are scared when it comes to the Middle East. Pastors have told me, "I'm looking around, and I'm so concerned by what I see." Why are they concerned? I'm not. God knows what He is doing. And if that's true, it is ridiculous for us to be afraid. God is in control of the Middle East, and He is in control of Israel. That alone should be enough to bring peace to our hearts, no matter how bad the craziness that we see on our television screens at night.

Not only should we not be afraid, we should be encouraged. Everything is playing out exactly as God said it would. The day is approaching. How do I know? Read Psalm 83. Read Ezekiel 36–37. Then look at the Middle East and Israel. By the fulfillment of prophecy and the actions of the nations, that whole region of the world is crying out, "Come, Lord Jesus, come!"

CHAPTER 9

WHEN THE RESTRAINER STOPS RESTRAINING

THE RAIN KEPT POURING DOWN. It had been days since south-central Pennsylvania had seen the sun. The trickles ran down hills, forming streams that turned into small rivers, all looking for pools where the water could stop its journey and accumulate. One of those collection pools was Lake Conemaugh—a reservoir created when the South Fork Dam was built in the mid-nineteenth century. Now, decades later, the poor engineering of the dam was about to reveal itself in a disastrous way.

On May 31, 1889, the constant downpour finally prevailed. The South Fork Dam burst, sending 3.8 billion gallons of water crashing down the mountain toward unsuspecting Johnstown, Pennsylvania. As the water rushed, it picked up debris—trees, cabins, railroad cars. It also swept up victims as it tore through helpless small towns—South Fork, Mineral Point, and East Conemaugh. When the flood finally reached Johnstown some 57 minutes later, the wall of water and wreckage was 35 feet high and travelling at 40 miles per hour. The destruction was unimaginable. A reported 2,209 people lost their lives that day, including 99 entire families wiped off the face of the earth.[1]

All that potential for destruction had been there for years, but it had been restrained by the dam. Once the restrainer was removed, devastation followed. This is the very picture that Paul presents in 2 Thessalonians 2. There is a restrainer in place right now, held secure by the Lord. But it will not remain there forever. A time is coming when the restrainer will be removed. On that day, people had better run for high ground, because devastation is about to pour down

THE COMING APOSTASY

Great confusion surrounds Paul's words in 2 Thessalonians 2. There is little doubt that he is talking about the end times and the coming of the Antichrist. It's the timing of the passage's events that creates the debate. The origin of the uncertainty resides less in Paul's words than in how people read them. Many, however, don't read as far as they should.

Paul began, "Now, brethren, concerning the coming of our Lord Jesus Christ and our gathering together to Him, we ask you, not to be soon shaken in mind or troubled, either by spirit or by word or by letter, as if from us, as though the day of Christ had come" (verses 1-2). A rumor was spreading, saying that Christ had returned, and the Thessalonians had somehow been left behind. Paul told them, "Don't worry, folks. It's all fake news." He encouraged them not to panic or rush to conclusions. There is an order of events that must occur before the return of Christ. The day is approaching, but it's not here yet.

Up to this point, everyone seems to agree on what is said in the passage. The problem comes when some people read just one more verse, then stop. This premature halt leaves them with a thoroughly wrong conclusion. Paul wrote, "Let no one deceive you by any means; for that Day will not come unless the falling away comes first" (2 Thessalonians 2:3). Jesus will not return until there is a falling away. The Greek word here is *apostasia*, which gives us the English word *apostasy*. There are some who say that this word refers to the rapture, which makes no sense linguistically or logically. Paul is not saying that the rapture will not happen until after the rapture happens. What if I decided to not write the next sentence until after I have written the next sentence. Oy, my head is starting to hurt just thinking about it.

Apostasy refers to false and wrong teachings that originate inside the church. There will always be false teachings outside in the world. But when heretical beliefs originate and spread within the family of God, then we are in real trouble. Sadly, this kind of apostasy is rampant in today's church.

There are constantly new movements popping up within the church that put the wrong emphasis on the wrong things. Health, wealth, signs, wonders, happiness, relevance—all are lures false teachers have used to hook people away from truth. One such spiritual deceiver is found in Davao City, the Philippines. Pastor Apollo Quiboloy calls himself the Appointed Son of God and teaches that he is the one through whom the Father rules His kingdom on earth.[2] If you go to his website, you will find plenty of information about him, his church, and how to "partner" with his ministry.[3] What you will not find is a doctrinal statement. Why? Because his doctrine fluctuates with his progressive revelations.

What a pain it would be to constantly have to update your website every time God changes His mind and comes up with a new truth. Besides, Quiboloy isn't about doctrine or the Bible or God; he is about himself. You may say, "Sure, Amir, there are meshugana preachers all over the place. Why focus on him?" Because Quiboloy claims to have 6 million followers in 200 countries—that's 6 million people led astray by a single deceiver.

How do people get caught up in deceptions like Quiboloy's? It's because they don't know their Bibles. When some Sadducees were trying to trip up Jesus with a hypothetical story about seven brothers successively marrying the same woman, Jesus called them out. "Are you not therefore mistaken, because you do not know the Scriptures nor the power of God?" (Mark 12:24). Deception is the product of ignorance. People are ignorant when they don't take time to learn. What should we be studying? The Word of God. It is our standard of truth. Do a preacher's words match the Bible? Then he is worth listening to. If not, he is part of the apostasy.

Paul told the Thessalonians not to become hysterical and worry that they may have been left behind. Before Jesus returns, there will come a great apostasy. After that, the time of the Antichrist will be ushered in.

> Let no one deceive you by any means; for that Day will not come unless the falling away comes first, and the man of sin is revealed, the son of perdition, who opposes and exalts himself above all that is called God or that is worshiped, so that he sits as God in the temple of God, showing himself that he is God (2 Thessalonians 2:3-4).

Many people stop reading there and say, "See, Amir, the rapture has to come at the end of the tribulation, because the Antichrist must be revealed first." Wait—keep reading.

Paul told the Thessalonians that yes, the son of perdition must be revealed. However, something else has to happen first: "Now you know what is restraining, that he may be revealed in his own time" (verse 6). Something is restraining, and something is being restrained. That's the first time this is mentioned. Let's read on: "For the mystery of lawlessness is already at work; only He who now restrains will do so until He is taken out of the way. And then the lawless one will be revealed" (verses 7-8). Notice the timing in these verses. Lawlessness is already at work. This is happening in the present time. The restraining one is now restraining and will continue to do so. However, at some point in the future, that restrainer will be removed, and the restraining will end. Once the restraining ends, the Antichrist will be revealed.

That's why we've got to read the whole passage. The best way to study the Bible is to let the Bible explain the Bible. Paul made it clear that there is one reason the Antichrist is not being revealed right this very moment: The restrainer has not yet been removed.

This brings up a question: What or who is the restrainer? In this chapter, we will address that question and others, including, What is he restraining? When did the restraining start? Why does the restrainer restrain? How does the restrainer restrain?

RESTRAINER REVEALED

Let's go on a journey of discovery. We'll begin with Adam, then move to Jesus, and finally to the Antichrist. Along this journey, we'll learn who this restrainer is, we'll see that he was around even back in the Old Testament, we'll get a picture of how he restrains, then we'll get a view of how all this plays out in the future.

From the moment sin first entered the world, judgment was required. Early in Genesis, we come to one of the most tragic portions of the Bible:

> The LORD saw that the wickedness of man was great in the earth, and that every intent of the thoughts of his heart was only evil continually. And the LORD was sorry that He had made man on the earth, and He was grieved in His heart. So the LORD said, "I will destroy man whom I have created from the face of the earth, both man and beast, creeping thing and birds of the air, for I am sorry that I have made them." But Noah found grace in the eyes of the LORD (Genesis 6:5-8).

God looked around and said, "Everything has gotten so unbelievably bad that I need to destroy it all." While this pronouncement is harsh, it is not wrong. We earn our punishment. "The wages of sin is death, but the gift of God is eternal life in Christ Jesus our Lord" (Romans 6:23). Humanity deserves all the punishment that is due, and we should have no expectation of anything else. Recently, I saw a Facebook post that showed an empty room. The caption read, "This room is full of all the people who deserve God's grace."

> God is not looking for an excuse to destroy; He is looking for an excuse to preserve and to bless.

Yet God does give grace. In both the Genesis passage and in Romans, the key word is "but." That one word changes everything. It is the most wonderful conjunction in the history of language. It says, "Although this is what you deserve, it's not what you're going to get." God is not looking for an excuse to destroy; He is looking for an excuse to preserve and to bless. "But Noah" introduces God's perfect grace into a humanity that had gone far off the rails. When you look at Noah's life, particularly after the flood, you see he wasn't all that great. He had a bit of a temper, and he liked to indulge in a little too much wine. However, he was good enough to preserve.

We are alive today because the Lord restrained His complete judgment of the world, leaving the window open for the wonderful mercy found in "But Noah."

God restrains. Satan, on the other hand, never restrains himself. From day one when he came in the form of a serpent, he was out to attack and destroy. Peter wrote, "Be sober, be vigilant; because your adversary the devil walks about like a roaring lion, seeking whom he may devour" (1 Peter 5:8). Satan never rests. He is always on his mission. When we let our guard down, that is when he will pounce and take us out.

When the Antichrist comes, there will be no inherent restraint in him either because he is following his master, the devil.

> The coming of the lawless one is according to the working of Satan, with all power, signs, and lying wonders, and with all unrighteous deception among those who perish, because they did not receive the love of the truth, that they might be saved. And for this reason God will send them strong delusion, that they should believe the lie, that they all may be condemned who did not believe the truth but had pleasure in unrighteousness (2 Thessalonians 2:9-12).

With the Antichrist comes godlessness and unrighteousness amongst the masses. His heinous actions will be welcomed by people with open arms. Why? Notice the word "because" in the passage above. The Antichrist's audience will be comprised of all those who did not receive "the love of the truth." That truth is the Word of God and the gospel contained within it. Receive that truth, and you will be saved. Reject that truth, and salvation will remain far from you.

It is this rejection that will lead the Lord to send strong delusions. These delusions won't pull the people away from the truth—they had already rejected it. God is a God of truth and Satan is the father of lies. People will have made their choice, and they will live with the consequences of being caught up in the confusion of the enemy's deceit. At first, however, there will be no sorrow in their rejection of the truth. Instead, there will be "pleasure in unrighteousness."

Those last three words in 2 Thessalonians 2:12 perfectly describe our world today. People love their sins. For many, their ignorance of the truth has so corrupted their minds that they don't even recognize sin as sin anymore. They'll say, "Don't give me the Bible; don't give me truth." They'll say,

- "I will determine truth, not you."
- "I will determine what male and female is, not you."
- "I will determine what a family is, not you."
- "I will determine my own sexual norms, not you."
- "I will do according to my pleasure, my rules, my law, my free will."

Some people won't like reading those words. I once had a woman come up to me and say, "Amir, why am I always so uncomfortable when you speak?" I don't know—sometimes the truth is uncomfortable. The Bible was not written to make us comfortable. Instead, it was given to show us who we are. Scripture is God's truth for addressing the sinful person we discover in the spiritual mirror. One surety we have is that the Bible will not tolerate sin and the deceptions of the devil just to make us feel better about ourselves.

Humanity can be divided into two groups: the condemned, and the not condemned. Jesus said,

> God did not send His Son into the world to condemn
> the world, but that the world through Him might be

saved. He who believes in Him is not condemned; but he who does not believe is condemned already, because he has not believed in the name of the only begotten Son of God. And this is the condemnation, that the light has come into the world, and men loved darkness rather than light, because their deeds were evil (John 3:17-19).

There are those who love the light and follow the Son. They are not condemned. But the others, the condemned, love darkness rather than the light. They reject the truth, and as a result, their fate is sealed. Leading this charge of deception away from the truth is Satan. He is in no way restrained from carrying out his hateful business.

If Satan is not the one being restrained, who or what is? For this answer, we need to look back to Abraham. God had seen the depraved condition of Sodom and Gomorrah reach a point that He decided to destroy those two towns. Before He did, He stopped for a meal at Abraham's tent. After dinner, as Abraham was walking along with this physical manifestation of God, the Lord revealed His intent to bring judgment on the sinful cities.

In response, Abraham proved he truly is the father of us Jews by initiating business negotiations with the Lord.

> Would You also destroy the righteous with the wicked? Suppose there were fifty righteous within the city; would You also destroy the place and not spare it for the fifty righteous that were in it? Far be it from You to do such a thing as this, to slay the righteous with the wicked, so that the righteous should be as the wicked; far be it from You! Shall not the Judge of all the earth do right? (Genesis 18:23-25).

The Lord, full of grace, told Abraham that for 50 righteous people, He would spare the city.

Abraham sensed an opportunity and went a step further. "Who am I to ask anything from You, but what if they're five short in the righteous people department?" The Lord assures him that 45 would be okay. Abraham counters back with 40. "Forty is fine," says the Lord. "Thirty…twenty…ten?" "I will not destroy it for the sake of ten," said the Lord (verse 32).

Notice God's patience through the negotiations. He had no obligation to give Abraham the time of day. Yet He let this mere human bargain with him. But that fits God's character. Abraham wasn't doing a bad thing. He was negotiating for the salvation of others. He was pleading for God to restrain His judgment. We can't miss this point. Who is acting as the restrainer here? Abraham stood in the role of one pleading for the Lord to hold back His judgment against the people. Restraint has everything to do with judgment— whether God carries out the judgment or delays it.

Another example is found in Job. Satan came to God and asked permission to give Job the works. Satan is all about killing and destroying and tearing apart. Again, there is no restraint at all in the devil. But Job's perspective is very different:

> Oh, that my words were written!
> Oh, that they were inscribed in a book!
> That they were engraved on a rock
> with an iron pen and lead, forever!
> For I know that my Redeemer lives,
> and He shall stand at last on the earth;
> and after my skin is destroyed, this I know,
> that in my flesh I shall see God…
> Be afraid of the sword for yourselves;
> for wrath brings the punishment of the sword,
> that you may know there is a judgment
> (Job 19:23-26,29).

Job was not afraid of Satan. He did not fear the enemy's attacks and schemes. What was it that frightened this righteous man? The judgment of God. Job knew that if there was one penalty that all of us deserve—whether you were a good person like himself or the worst person on earth—it is judgment from the Lord as just recompense for our sins. "All we like sheep have gone astray; we have turned, every one, to his own way; and the LORD has laid on Him the iniquity of us all" (Isaiah 53:6). Our sins brought us death. Then came the Lamb—the Savior of mankind. In Jesus, the solution for our sin had been provided.

From Adam onward, the problem of sin affects everyone. And, because of that sin, judgment is required. That is why Jesus came into the world:

> At the end of the ages, [Christ] has appeared to put away sin by the sacrifice of Himself. And as it is appointed for men to die once, but after this the judgment, so Christ was offered once to bear the sins of many. To those who eagerly wait for Him He will appear a second time, apart from sin, for salvation (Hebrews 9:26-28).

What is the salvation spoken of here? It is the Romans 8:18-25 salvation of our bodies from this world at Jesus' return. He will come back, but this time it will not be to offer Himself for our sins. That's been taken care of. When He returns, He will save us out of this world. That is worth eagerly waiting for! Before Jesus, we were awaiting our judgment from God with dread. Now, we are excitedly anticipating His return.

Finally, we come to the identity of the restrainer. God's judgment is ready for this world. However, He is holding it back until the time is right and He removes His church. Thus, the restrainer is God's presence in His people who are in this world. We are His ambassadors. We are His watchmen. When people see us, they see Christ. And when they see Christ, they see the Father.

When people see us, they see Christ. And when they see Christ, they see the Father.

If the Father has restraining powers over His judgment, then that means we are the embodiment of the restraining power of God. As long as we are here on earth, God will restrain His judgment. But when we are gone, His judgment will burst forth like the floodwaters from the South Fork Dam.

THE CHURCH'S ROLE IN RESTRAINING

In the Sermon on the Mount, Jesus said, "You are the salt of the earth; but if the salt loses its flavor, how shall it be seasoned? It is then good for nothing but to be thrown out and trampled underfoot by men" (Matthew 5:13). What does salt do? It slows down decay. This is our role on the earth. The only reason the world has not fallen completely into sin and ultimate judgment is because we are here to slow down the decline. If the church doesn't do its part in this world, then what good are we? We must intentionally be Christ to the people around us, restraining the judgment of God as He allows us.

Believers are the face of God to this world. Jesus said, "If you had known Me, you would have known My Father also; and from now on you know Him and have seen Him" (John 14:7). You don't have to be the Father to show people the Father. God is not in temples made by men; God is in men made to be His temple.

Paul, as he stood before the intellectual elite in Athens, said, "God, who made the world and everything in it, since He is Lord of heaven and earth, does not dwell in temples made with hands. Nor is He worshiped with men's hands, as though He needed anything, since He gives to all life, breath, and all things" (Acts 17:24-25). God is not in temples made by human hands; He is in temples that are made by His hands. Paul wrote to the Corinthians, "Do you not know that your body is the temple of the Holy Spirit who is in you, whom you have from God, and you are not your own?" (1 Corinthians 6:19). We are the temples in which He dwells. So when the world sees us, they see Jesus. And when they see Jesus, they see the Father.

Our very presence in this world is what restrains the judgment that is yet to come. "Beloved, do not forget this one thing, that with the Lord one day is as a thousand years, and a thousand years as one day. The Lord is not slack concerning His promise, as some count slackness, but is longsuffering toward us, not willing that any should perish but that all should come to repentance" (2 Peter 3:8-9). We remain on this earth because the Lord is long-suffering. That's the God we serve. That's the God we love.

Paul wrote to Timothy that we should pray for all those in authority over us so that we may lead quiet, peaceable lives (1 Timothy 2:1-2). He then said, "This is good and acceptable in the sight of God our Savior, who desires all men to be saved and to come to the knowledge of the truth" (verses 3-4). God desires that all come to salvation, but this is utterly their choice. He has offered the free gift, but it must be accepted to be of any use.

If you haven't yet, receive the gift. That's all God is asking of you. Accept Jesus as your Savior and Lord—make Him number one in your life. It's that simple. God wants you to be part of His family, and He wants you to want to be part of His family. He could have forced or coerced or tricked you. Instead, He straightforwardly put out the option. Choose God and receive life; reject God and receive death.

As long as the restrainer—God in us—remains in this world, the option is still open for those who have not received Him. However, as 2 Thessalonians tells us, there will come a day when the restrainer is removed. During the tribulation, few will search for the Lord because deceit from Satan will be so prevalent. Now is the day of our salvation. Today, before it is too late.

THE REMOVAL OF THE RESTRAINER

We have seen what the restrainer is—God's presence in the church. We have also seen what the restrainer is holding back—the Lord's judgment upon the world. When the church is removed, there will be nothing left to hold back the powerful, evil force of the enemy.

How will the restrainer be removed? We've already seen the answer to this question in 1 Thessalonians:

> The Lord Himself will descend from heaven with a shout, with the voice of an archangel, and with the trumpet of God. And the dead in Christ will rise first. Then we who are alive and remain shall be caught up together with them in the clouds to meet the Lord in the air. And thus we shall always be with the Lord. Therefore comfort one another with these words (4:16-18).

God will physically remove the restrainer from the earth. Once the Lord raptures His church to be with Him in the air, this will usher in the next phase of God's plan.

If the church is such a moderating presence—holding back the wrath of God as we shine the light of Christ—then why would the Lord want to remove us? Why doesn't He just extend His patience with the world by keeping us here? Because judgment must come. There is a soon-coming moment when the spiritual clock hands will reach 12:00 and the alarm will go off. In 2 Peter 3:8-9, we saw that the

Lord is long-suffering, not wanting anyone to perish. What a wonderful show of God's grace! Yet notice the first word in verse 10—"but."

> But the day of the Lord will come as a thief in the night, in which the heavens will pass away with a great noise, and the elements will melt with fervent heat; both the earth and the works that are in it will be burned up (2 Peter 3:10).

The Lord is patient, but a time will come when His patience ends and judgment falls.

Mankind deserves the penalty that is soon approaching, yet even in the midst of pouring out judgment, the Lord will still be at work drawing people to Himself. God has a higher purpose for the tribulation—a purpose that runs beyond punishment. That horrible time of testing is specifically designed for Israel's salvation.

"But, Amir, is God really going to cause so much havoc just so Israel can be saved?" Through the prophet Hosea, the Lord said, "I will return again to My place till they acknowledge their offense. Then they will seek My face; in their affliction they will earnestly seek Me" (5:15). How sad it is that we tend to seek God only when things are at their worst. When life is going well, we tend to go about our business and ignore the God who gave our circumstances their present "okay-ness." Frequently it is pain that gets us to turn our eyes up to God. It takes affliction for us to drop to our knees before Him.

READING THE SIGNS

On that day when the restrainer is removed, God will usher in His wrath upon sinful mankind. Yet He will also use the judgments of the tribulation to get His chosen people to return to Him.

This brings us to the final question: When will the restrainer be removed? According to 2 Thessalonians 2, just before the Antichrist is revealed. When we see the signs of the Antichrist's rise all around us, then the rapture of the church is imminent. And when the church is raptured, the restrainer will be taken from this world.

What do today's signs tell us? Can we expect that the Antichrist will be revealed soon?

The answer is an emphatic *yes*.

CHAPTER 10

MEANWHILE, UP IN HEAVEN...

LET ME CLUE YOU IN ON A LITTLE SECRET—I don't mind flying. I know that the popular take is for people to complain about how miserable air travel is, but I'm not one of them. Sure, the check-in lines are long, and there is the hassle of getting through security—you haven't truly been through that until you've experienced Israel's airport security checks. Then you have to deal with expensive airport food, the cramped seating on the planes, and the less-than-stellar quality of those high-priced rewarmed meals.

But there is one experience in air travel that makes enduring all the problems worthwhile. It's that moment when the plane breaks through the top of the clouds. Above you is blue sky as far as you can see; below is a white barrier separating you from all that's taking place on terra firma. Atop the clouds are peace and beauty; underneath the clouds are violence and hatred and sorrow. We might even get a sad feeling when the plane breaks the lower surface of the clouds because it means we are descending back to the chaos below.

I not only find joy above the cloud line; I also experience it while I am within the clouds themselves. When the plane is cruising through the thick masses of water droplets and moisture beads make their way across the window panes, I'm smiling. I'm thinking of the future. I dream of the day when I will be inside the clouds yet outside of the plane. That is where I will meet my Lord face to face for the first time. Then, after I am gathered with the rest of the church on that blessed day and we are received by the Savior, we will go up with Him, and not come back down. Seven years will go by before we'll see the surface of the earth again. During that time, there is a lot that will be taking place below the clouds, as well as above.

Most books dealing with the end times focus mainly on what is going to happen on the earth during the tribulation. I get that—it's fascinating to see how God's future plans for the world will unfold. In my previous book, *The Last Hour*, I spent a fair amount of time talking about the Antichrist and those seven years on earth. But ultimately, what's happening below the clouds has little to do with what we're going to be experiencing above. And that is really where our minds ought to be—on the things above.

SET YOUR MIND ON THINGS ABOVE

In his letter to the Colossians, Paul wrote, "If then you were raised with Christ, seek those things which are above, where Christ is, sitting at the right hand of God. Set your mind on things above, not on things on the earth" (Colossians 3:1-2). Our minds should not be first and foremost on the cares of the earth, but on what is above.

By "above," Paul was not talking about the moon and the stars. There are many who are fascinated by the heavens above us. Some use the stars and constellations to create horoscopes in the foolish belief that the various alignments of the heavenly bodies can give them insight into their character and future. Others are simply fascinated with outer space, wanting to look as deeply as they can into the universe to marvel at its expanses, gain scientific insights, or meet and greet other forms of life. There is nothing wrong with studying the heavens—they are all part of the beautiful vastness of God's creation. But to seek other creatures in space rather than the Creator of space is to miss the very point of God's creation.

Paul said that if we have been raised with Christ, then the things that are above should be our main concern. When we turn on the television, it's difficult not to become preoccupied with the things of the world. Hostilities are everywhere. There are wars and violence all around the globe. Societies are deteriorating amid the onslaught of secularism, postmodernism, abortion, gender issues, immorality, and so much more. Our minds must not be dragged down by these concerns.

That doesn't mean we should ignore the world—not at all. As the church, we must take our stand for truth and for life. But we do so with our eyes looking up. We do so as ambassadors for Christ, living His truth and love to this dying generation. Through it all, we must remember that ultimately, this world is not our home.

We cannot shift our vision from downward to upward on our own. We will not be able to seek the things above, according to Paul, unless something happens first. According to Colossians 3:1, we must be "raised with Christ." "But, Amir, don't I have to be dead first in order to be raised?" Yes, most definitely. And if you have not been raised with Christ, then as you are reading this, you are stone-cold dead. "But, Amir, if I am dead, then how…?" Stop right there. I understand your confusion. The answer to your question is in the first two words of verse 1: "If then…"

When reading the Bible, anytime you come across the words "If then," that indicates you need to stop your forward progress and put yourself into reverse. Those two words typically direct you backward to a point that the author has just made. For this passage, we must slide back to the previous chapter, where Paul penned these words:

> In Him you were also circumcised with the circumcision made without hands, by putting off the body of the sins of the flesh, by the circumcision of Christ, buried with Him in baptism, in which you also were raised with Him through faith in the working of God, who raised Him from the dead. And you, being dead in your trespasses and the uncircumcision of your flesh, He has made alive together with Him, having forgiven you all trespasses, having wiped out the handwriting of requirements that was against us, which was contrary to us. And He has taken it out of the way, having nailed it to the cross (Colossians 2:11-14).

In the previous chapter, we read that "the wages of sin is death" (Romans 6:23). Here, Paul reminds us of that same truth—before salvation, we were "dead in [our] trespasses." Even though we were physically alive, we were spiritually doornail dead. But Christ, through His work on the cross, has forgiven all our sins and dealt with the penalty that was due to us. Now, "through faith in the working of God," we are raised with Christ. This resurrected life is what makes us a new creation.

Once we are new creations, everything changes. We now have the capacity to comprehend that the things of this world are not what life is all about. So many people try to live their lives with one leg in the world and one leg in the Word. But that never works. Anyone who tries that will inevitably fall onto the worldly leg. When we are made new, our thinking completely changes. Paul said that "our citizenship is in heaven, from which we also eagerly wait for the Savior, the Lord Jesus Christ" (Philippians 3:20).

We belong to our new kingdom. Here on earth, we are illegal

immigrants because we've surrendered our citizenship. That is why the world hates the church. Jesus said, "If you were of the world, the world would love its own. Yet because you are not of the world, but I chose you out of the world, therefore the world hates you" (John 15:19). We can endure the antipathy of this present age, however, because our eyes are looking above.

FROM CORRUPTIBLE TO INCORRUPTIBLE

What are we to focus on when we look up? A better question is this: Upon *whom* should we focus? Our eyes should be on "Christ who died, and furthermore is also risen, who is even at the right hand of God, who also makes intercession for us" (Romans 8:34). Jesus, who lived on this earth, died on the cross, and rose again on the third day is now sitting at the right hand of the Father.

How do we know this? The Bible tells us. Not enough for you? We also have an eyewitness. When Stephen was about to be stoned for preaching Christ, "he, being full of the Holy Spirit, gazed into heaven and saw the glory of God, and Jesus standing at the right hand of God, and said, 'Look! I see the heavens opened and the Son of Man standing at the right hand of God!'" (Acts 7:55-56). Stephen saw into the throne room of God. Then moments later, he was standing in that very throne room. Because we are new creations, we are able to put our full focus on Jesus, who is in heaven with the Father.

How did Jesus get from here to there? After His resurrection, He spent time with the disciples. Then the day came for Him to leave.

> When He had spoken these things, while they watched, He was taken up, and a cloud received Him out of their sight. And while they looked steadfastly toward heaven as He went up, behold, two men stood by them in white apparel, who also said, "Men of Galilee, why do you

stand gazing up into heaven? This same Jesus, who was taken up from you into heaven, will so come in like manner as you saw Him go into heaven" (Acts 1:9-11).

Jesus was taken up into a cloud, and that was the last the disciples saw of Him. As they stood there with their jaws hanging open, angels came and told them, "Yeah, this looks kind of weird, but get used to it. He's coming back the same way."

How did Jesus go up? He was "taken up." That sounds like what we read in 1 Thessalonians 4:15-17 and 1 Corinthians 15:51-53. We will be changed, then we will be taken up to meet Jesus in those wonderful clouds. The primary difference between the two events is the speed at which they take place. The disciples were able to watch Jesus ascend. But when we go, it will be like when you push the button on your remote to make the recording go 4x speed. Jesus gradually lifted off, but we'll be gone in the blink of an eye.

Aren't you looking forward to that change? I certainly am. First Corinthians describes the transformation this way:

> Behold, I tell you a mystery: We shall not all sleep, but we shall all be changed—in a moment, in the twinkling of an eye, at the last trumpet. For the trumpet will sound, and the dead will be raised incorruptible, and we shall be changed. For this corruptible must put on incorruption, and this mortal must put on immortality (1 Corinthians 15:51-53).

We are living in lowly bodies that are slowly decaying. Want proof? Take a look at a picture of yourself 20 years ago. See any difference? If you don't, it's probably because you know a very high-priced plastic surgeon out of Hollywood. We are corruptible, and we are corrupting. But that is okay—it's nothing to get upset about because we've got a new, upgraded body waiting for us.

In that moment when we are taken to be with our Savior, we will say *adios* to the corruptible and *hello* to incorruption—we will say *good-bye* to the mortal and *shalom* to immortality. Our body cells won't decay anymore. Sickness won't bother us anymore. We won't be able to die anymore. When we leave this earth, our resurrected bodies will finally catch up with our resurrected souls. And then, we will be with our Savior.

As we saw in the last chapter, when the restrainer is removed, we will rise to meet Jesus. We will finally go home to the kingdom of our citizenship—to the place above, where our minds have been firmly set.

This raises the next logical question: What will happen once we get there?

SEVEN YEARS IN HEAVEN

We are raptured from this earth. We see the face of our Savior. We rise with Him to heaven. What then? Seven years will go by before we return with Jesus at the second coming. While all the turmoil is happening below, what will be taking place above? Like a beautifully wrapped present waiting for Christmas morning, the Lord leaves most of that time as a mystery to us. However, there are three events that we know will take place.

Your Room Is Ready

I believe that the first activity will be the distribution of the places that Jesus has prepared for us. Admittedly, this is speculation based on what I read in the Bible, and I promise you that I will let you know when I am presenting such. In the upper room, Jesus told the disciples, "In My Father's house are many mansions; if it were not so, I would have told you. I go to prepare a place for you. And if I go and prepare a place for you, I will come again and receive you to Myself; that where I am, there you may be also" (John 14:2-3).

When I am leading a tour and the bus pulls up at a hotel, the first thing that we must do is check in. Unfortunately, that's not always an easy process. The lines can be long. People can wander off to look at the sites. Often what should be a quick process seems to take forever. Similarly, with all the people arriving in heaven with Christ at the same time, just the check-in time could take the full seven years. The line could be miles long. However, I'm guessing that God has figured out a better process than what I typically encounter with one hotel clerk trying to fix his or her computer, one clerk wandering off on a cigarette break, and one clerk actually checking people in.

> No one wants to see your joy and wonderment more than your Savior. Imagine what He has in store for you!

Are you excited about seeing the wonderful place that Christ has prepared for you? No one knows you better. No one loves you more. No one wants to see your joy and wonderment more than your Savior. Imagine what He has in store for you!

Passing Out the Prizes

While the first event in heaven is an educated guess based on Scripture, the second is explicitly spoken of. Paul wrote about this to the Corinthians:

> We are confident, yes, well pleased rather to be absent from the body and to be present with the Lord. Therefore we make it our aim, whether present or absent, to be well pleasing to Him. For we must all appear before the judgment seat of Christ, that each one may receive the

things done in the body, according to what he has done, whether good or bad (2 Corinthians 5:8-10).

There will come a time during those seven years when the entire raptured church will gather together before Christ. The Greek word translated "judgment seat" is *bema*. In ancient Roman culture, the bema seat was an elevated platform on which a government official or judge would sit. At times, the bema seat was a place where disputes and court cases were adjudicated. It also saw action during competitive events. When someone was victorious in a contest or race, that person would stand before the bema. There, an official would give him or her a reward. Typically, the prize was a *stephanos*, a crown made of woven branches.

Whenever you read in the New Testament of crowns being given to people, such as Paul's crown of righteousness in 2 Timothy 4:8 or the elders' crowns that are laid before the Lord's throne in Revelation 4:10, these are always the *stephanos* crown. They are crowns of victory and reward, not of position or title. However, when Christ returns riding His white horse, He will not be wearing mere woven branches. On His head will sit the *diadem*—a crown of royalty fit for the King of kings and Lord of lords (Revelation 19:11-16).

When we stand before the bema, we will do so for both judgment and reward. The judgment we face, however, is not regarding our salvation. If you have made it to heaven, you will stay in heaven. There is no trap door in the floor that will open down to Hades if Christ finds you lacking. Instead, we will be judged for our intentions—the motivations we had when we carried out our service for Christ.

No other foundation can anyone lay than that which is laid, which is Jesus Christ. Now if anyone builds on this foundation with gold, silver, precious stones, wood, hay, straw, each one's work will become clear; for the Day will declare it, because it will be revealed by fire; and the fire will test each one's work, of what sort it is. If anyone's work which he has built on it endures, he will receive a reward. If anyone's work is burned, he will suffer loss; but he himself will be saved, yet so as through fire (1 Corinthians 3:11-15).

As the crowd gathers around and we take our turn in front of the judgment seat, all our works for the Lord will be read out. Then they'll be torched. All that was done out of selfishness or pride or personal gain will go up in smoke. All that was done out of sacrifice and mercy and grace—everything done out of love for God and for others—will stand up under the fire. It is for these good works that Jesus will reach down from His seat and place the *stephanos* crowns on our heads. Imagine the joy you will feel when the woven branches are gently pressed down and you hear the voice of your Savior saying, "Well done, good and faithful servant."

For us to experience that reward and not stand there embarrassed without a crown, we need to be intentional about our lives and our service today. Paul compares this focused life to a runner who dedicates himself to obtaining an earthly crown. This runner goes into training and is careful about how he treats his body. Paul's point is that if people can be that dedicated to getting a leafy wreath that will eventually rot away, how much more should we be committed to winning crowns that will last forever. He said, "Run in such a way that you may obtain it...Therefore I run thus: not with uncertainty. Thus I fight: not as one who beats the air. But I discipline my body and bring it into subjection" (1 Corinthians 9:24,26-27). This means living a life of sacrifice and holiness.

Paul presented to believers a very high bar for this kind of life. For example, he wrote, "Husbands, love your wives, just as Christ also loved the church and gave Himself for her, that He might sanctify and cleanse her with the washing of water by the word, that He might present her to Himself a glorious church, not having spot or wrinkle or any such thing, but that she should be holy and without blemish" (Ephesians 5:25-27). Although this is written in the context of marriage, it speaks of the kind of determined love we should show in all our relationships. Christ's love for the church set the standard we should strive for. When we live with this kind of other-centered, self-sacrificial love, all that is set on fire before the bema seat will withstand the flames.

In the Ephesians passage, Paul gave another reason given for why it's essential that we be committed to righteousness. Christ is determined to have a bride who is spotless, holy, and without blemish. In other words, as we strive for godly living and wash ourselves daily with the Word of God, we are preparing ourselves to meet our bridegroom. This preparation is essential so that we are ready when He comes.

Jesus told a parable about ten virgins who were waiting for their bridegroom to come take them away. He began, "The kingdom of heaven shall be likened to ten virgins who took their lamps and went out to meet the bridegroom. Now five of them were wise, and five were foolish. Those who were foolish took their lamps and took no oil with them" (Matthew 25:1-3). All ten appeared to be ready on the outside, but five of them were actually in trouble. They had left home without oil for their lamps. There are many professing Christians in churches today who are waiting for Christ to return, but they don't have the Holy Spirit—the oil. They go through the forms of Christianity, but there is nothing in their lamps. They have never made a commitment to truly follow Christ. They were never raised from death to life, so their eyes are not truly on the things above.

When Jesus comes to take His church, He will catch these people unaware the same way the bridegroom caught the five oil-less virgins unaware. As the true bride leaves this earth with His followers, the others will be left behind.

That is why as we wait for Christ's return, we must prepare ourselves to meet Him. That begins with making sure that you have made yourself right with the Lord by accepting His free gift of salvation through faith. When you do that, the Holy Spirit will fill your lamp to overflowing.

A Royal Wedding

If the church is taken up to be the bride of Christ, then that tells us there's a wedding waiting to happen. That is the third great event that will occur during those seven years God is pouring out His wrath on the earth:

> "Let us be glad and rejoice and give Him glory, for the marriage of the Lamb has come, and His wife has made herself ready." And to her it was granted to be arrayed in fine linen, clean and bright, for the fine linen is the righteous acts of the saints. Then he said to me, "Write: 'Blessed are those who are called to the marriage supper of the Lamb!'" And he said to me, "These are the true sayings of God" (Revelation 19:7-9).

Not long ago, the world watched as Prince William married Kate Middleton, and later, Prince Harry wed Meghan Markle. The brides were beautiful, and royal pageantry was on full display. Just think what the wedding of Christ to His bride will look like. Royal-watchers will be going nuts.

Prior to William or Harry marrying their duchesses, did they send them through a trial by ordeal so that they would prove themselves worthy? Were the brides forced to endure a period of suffering and pain to purify themselves from any commonness left in them?

Of course not. What kind of a groom would do such a thing? But that is essentially what those who believe in a post-tribulation rapture are espousing. They have Christ saying, "My dear bride, I would love to marry you now, but you're just not quite up to par yet. Maybe seven years in the tribulational meat grinder will do the trick."

There are two fatal flaws to the post-trib argument. The first is the belief that the church is not quite worthy yet to marry the Savior. The truth is that we are 100 percent ready because it is Jesus who has made us worthy. "[God] made Him who knew no sin to be sin for us, that we might become the righteousness of God in Him" (2 Corinthians 5:21). We are not fit to be the bride of Christ because of anything that we have done. We are marriage material purely because of what He has done for us.

> We are not fit to be the bride of Christ because of anything that we have done. We are marriage material purely because of what He has done for us.

The second flaw is that Jesus has promised to spare us from the coming wrath. To the church in Philadelphia, Jesus proclaimed, "Because you have kept My command to persevere, I also will keep you from the hour of trial which shall come upon the whole world, to test those who dwell on the earth" (Revelation 3:10). Notice the word "from." It is not the word "through" or "in." The promise is that the church will be kept "from" that hour or trial. And that makes sense. The purpose of the trial is to "test those who dwell on the earth."

Why does the church need to be tested? To find out how well we can take a punch? Because we have been justified, we are already tested and approved through the blood of Jesus Christ. "For God did not appoint us to wrath, but to obtain salvation through our

Lord Jesus Christ, who died for us, that whether we wake or sleep, we should live together with Him. Therefore comfort each other and edify one another, just as you also are doing" (1 Thessalonians 5:9-11). We are not appointed to suffer wrath. That is a message we can encourage one another with. If you want to stick around and ride out the tribulation, then be my guest. I've got a wedding to go to.

RETURNING BACK TO EARTH

This brings us to the end of our initial seven years in heaven. We will have moved into the places Christ prepared for us, we will have stood on trial and received our rewards, and we will have gotten ourselves a new husband. After that, it will be time for us to head back to earth. "Thus the LORD my God will come, and all the saints with You" (Zechariah 14:5). The Lord is returning, and we're coming with Him.

Now it's possible that after seven glorious years in heaven, we'll be saying, "Grrr! I don't want to come back to earth." But when we return, this place won't be like it was before because we won't be like we were before. We'll be coming back in our glorified bodies, sleek and lean and not needing our glasses, medicines, or any of that Slim-Fit stuff anymore.

And what will we do after we return? That is what the next three chapters are about.

CHAPTER 11

THE MILLENNIUM— THE THOUSAND YEARS BEGIN

A NUMBER OF YEARS BACK, there was a television advertising campaign for a drink called Nestea. Typically, the commercial would begin out in the hot summer sun. In that sweltering weather would be a man operating a jackhammer or a husband and wife moving furniture into a new home, or a group of young people vigorously playing volleyball on the beach. The one thing they all had in common was that sweat was pouring out of them like water from a squeezed sponge. Nearing dehydration, they would reach into a cooler full of ice and pull out a bottle of Nestea iced tea. After cracking open the bottle and taking a long drink, they would fall backward into a cool, refreshing pool that had miraculously appeared out of nowhere. As the people surfaced in the water with a long, satisfied sigh, the background music would reach a crescendo and the words "Take the Nestea Plunge" would flash across the screen.

In the previous chapter, we reached the end of the worst period of time this world will ever see—wars, death, plagues, and natural disasters on a scale that will leave the remaining few survivors reeling. They will desperately need refreshment and a long sigh of relief. Thankfully, God will have just what they're looking for. He will open up a global pool for all of creation to fall back into. There will be a long, collective "aaaahhhhhh" as God's wrath ends. Then a time of peace unseen since the garden will begin. This will be our introduction to the millennium.

"Wait, Amir—the millennium? Isn't this book called *The Day Approaching*? Seems to me that the Day has not only approached, but it's now past." Yes and no. The rapture has come and gone—that was a Day of the Lord. The seven years of Jacob's trouble has come and gone—they were a Day of the Lord. The second coming of the Messiah has seen the feet of Jesus on the Mount of Olives—that was a Day of the Lord. However, there is still one more Day to come. This will be a day of judgment, when all mankind will stand before the holy throne. The books will be opened, and if anyone's name is not found written in the Book of Life, they will be thrown into the lake of fire for all eternity. Between the second coming of the Messiah and that final day of judgment is a 1,000-year period known as the millennium.

There is good news and bad news when it comes to the millennium. The good news is that it is wonderful beyond our imagination. Peace and tranquility will be the new world order as Christ reigns from Jerusalem. The bad news is that we aren't in the millennium yet. Or, come to think of it, that could be good news too. There are many who say that we are in the millennium now. If we are, then I am very disappointed. It sounded so much better in the Bible.

It's like sitting through a mediocre movie after the previews promised so much more. Could this present world around us be all there is to the millennium? To determine whether we are in fact living in the 1,000-year reign of Christ, we need to separate ourselves from what traditions and denominations say and go right to the source.

The millennium is spoken of in both the Old and New Testaments. The apostle John wrote of what he witnessed regarding the onset of this period of peace:

> I saw an angel coming down from heaven, having the key to the bottomless pit and a great chain in his hand. He laid hold of the dragon, that serpent of old, who is the Devil and Satan, and bound him for a thousand years; and he cast him into the bottomless pit, and shut him up, and set a seal on him, so that he should deceive the nations no more till the thousand years were finished. But after these things he must be released for a little while.
>
> And I saw thrones, and they sat on them, and judgment was committed to them. Then I saw the souls of those who had been beheaded for their witness to Jesus and for the word of God, who had not worshiped the beast or his image, and had not received his mark on their foreheads or on their hands. And they lived and reigned with Christ for a thousand years. But the rest of the dead did not live again until the thousand years were finished. This is the first resurrection. Blessed and holy is he who has part in the first resurrection. Over such the second death has no power, but they shall be priests of God and of Christ, and shall reign with Him a thousand years (Revelation 20:1-6).

The "thousand years" that are spoken of is the source of the millennium's name—the Latin word for "thousand" is *mille*. As John tells us above, during this 1,000-year time, Satan will be cast into a bottomless pit. This long-deserved punishment will begin at the end of the tribulation. God will bind the devil, throw him in the pit, and slam the lid shut, sealing it so that there can be no prison breaks. Satan will be captive and his influence removed from the earth for the full 1,000 years. During that time, no one can say "The devil made me do it" because the deceit and destruction of the enemy will no longer be a direct force on the inhabitants of the earth. God promises us an entirely Satan-free environment, until…

That word "until" or "till" in Revelation 20:3 is key. This is both a promise and a warning. There is coming a period of time when the world will be free from satanic influence, but that time will be limited. John wrote, "[God] cast [the devil] into the bottomless pit…that he should deceive the nations no more till the thousand years were finished. But after these things he must be released for a little while" (Revelation 20:3). When the 1,000 years are up, Satan "must" be released. That word "must" is also key. For God to accomplish His plan, the prison door must open and Satan must get his walking papers. Then the world will enter a brief period of final testing. We will learn more about that later.

CHARACTERISTICS OF THE MILLENNIAL KINGDOM

For many, what they know about the millennium consists of lions and lambs and everybody basically getting along. But the Bible lays out much more detail about these 1,000 years. Through careful study, we can learn what the world will look like politically, spiritually, and with regard to nature. We can also conclude that it is simply impossible to be true to Scripture while still believing that we are currently living in the millennial kingdom. Here are some key reasons we can be certain we're not in the millennium.

From a Political Perspective

No Justice, No Peace

As we read about the political state of the earth during the millennium, we first see that the Lord's rule will be worldwide. Isaiah wrote, "It shall come to pass in the latter days that the mountain of the LORD's house shall be established on the top of the mountains, and shall be exalted above the hills; and all nations shall flow to it" (Isaiah 2:2). All people everywhere will be ruled by one King who reigns in one location. Today, there are between 193 to 197 countries in the world, depending on whom you ask. Each one of these nations has its own political system with its own rulers. During the millennium, there will be a one-world government, and its capital will be Jerusalem.

At that time, the earth will be peaceful. Again, we turn to Isaiah: "He shall judge between the nations, and rebuke many people; they shall beat their swords into plowshares, and their spears into pruning hooks; nation shall not lift up sword against nation, neither shall they learn war anymore" (Isaiah 2:4). Ummm…hello? Do we have a peaceful reign over all the earth? In truth, there is anything but. Nations are rising up against nations. Every newscast leads off with another threat from Russia or North Korea or Iran or Turkey. Sin and corruption are everywhere. We are a far cry from the promised righteousness and justice that will mark the millennium.

> With righteousness He shall judge the poor, and decide with equity for the meek of the earth; He shall strike the earth with the rod of His mouth, and with the breath of His lips He shall slay the wicked. Righteousness shall be the belt of His loins, and faithfulness the belt of His waist (Isaiah 11:4-5).

As we look around at the nations of this world, *righteousness* would not be the first word that pops into our minds.

No Temple, No Throne

The next characteristic of the millennium is clearly spelled out for us in Isaiah 2: "Many people shall come and say, 'Come, and let us go up to the mountain of the LORD, to the house of the God of Jacob; He will teach us His ways, and we shall walk in His paths.' For out of Zion shall go forth the law, and the word of the LORD from Jerusalem" (verse 3). The Lord's throne will be in the city of Jerusalem because He will reign from the throne of David. As one who lives in Israel, I spend a lot of time in Jerusalem. I can guarantee you that if the Lord had a throne right now in the city and He was ruling from it, I would likely know about it. That's not something easily hidden. Nor is that meant to be hidden. The Jews don't even have the Temple Mount, let alone a world-ruling throne room.

This future kingdom's political system will not be a democracy or a republic, but a theocracy. *Theos* means "God." Thus, in the millennium, the Lord Himself will be the government and the ruler. "Your eyes will see the King in His beauty; they will see the land that is very far off...For the LORD is our Judge, the LORD is our Lawgiver, the LORD is our King; He will save us" (Isaiah 33:17,22). Again, that is certainly not what we have today. It seems that if there is any great ruler in our current culture, it is the supreme courts. Frequently they have the final say over what the other branches of government attempt to do.

If God is the King, then it makes sense that His children are princes. "Behold, a king will reign in righteousness, and princes will rule with justice" (Isaiah 32:1). I don't know about you, but I'm certainly not ruling as a prince. No one is bowing down to me, and it has been quite a while since I tried on a crown.

No Supreme Israel

The final political characteristic of the millennium has to do with the nation of Israel. Because Israel will be the home of the

Lord's throne room in Jerusalem, it will be the supreme nation of the world. "'In the shadow of His hand He has hidden Me, and made Me a polished shaft; in His quiver He has hidden Me.' And He said to me, 'You are My servant, O Israel, in whom I will be glorified'" (Isaiah 49:2-3). Israel is a growing power in today's world, but it is not the premier superpower. That honor belongs to the United States. After that comes China, then Russia. But when the Lord sits on His throne in Jerusalem, all eyes will turn to Israel.

> Imagine a time when all the world will gather together to witness God's glory—a sight granted to only a select few in times past.

From a Spiritual Perspective

What will be the spiritual state of the world during the millennium? First, the glory and holiness of the Lord will be manifest. God speaks of that day when His glory will be seen by all: "I know their works and their thoughts. It shall be that I will gather all nations and tongues; and they shall come and see My glory" (Isaiah 66:18). Imagine a time when all the world will gather together to witness God's glory—a sight granted to only a select few in times past. In those coming days, an attitude of joy and praise will prevail amongst the people and there will be a general state of holiness throughout the Lord's creation.

The millennium will see the joyful return of all of God's chosen people to the Holy Land. "The ransomed of the LORD shall return, and come to Zion with singing, with everlasting joy on their heads. They shall obtain joy and gladness, and sorrow and sighing shall flee away" (Isaiah 35:10). This generation has seen the return of many of the Jews to the Promised Land. However, this has not been accompanied by universal joy and gladness. *Sigh* is the Jews' middle name. Even the cows, when they produce milk, sigh, "Oy vey."

During the millennium, Jerusalem will be the political center of the world and a rebuilt temple will serve as the worship center of the world. The Lord promises in Isaiah,

> Also the sons of the foreigner who join themselves to the LORD, to serve Him, and to love the name of the LORD, to be His servants—everyone who keeps from defiling the Sabbath, and holds fast My covenant—even them I will bring to My holy mountain, and make them joyful in My house of prayer. Their burnt offerings and their sacrifices will be accepted on My altar; for My house shall be called a house of prayer for all nations (Isaiah 56:6-7).

As I mentioned earlier, I am in Jerusalem quite often. When I stand on the Mount of Olives looking down on the Temple Mount, I see the Dome of the Rock, the al-Aqsa Mosque, and the Dome of the Chain. One structure that I do not see is the holy temple of the one true God.

There is another spiritual change that will overtake the city of Jerusalem, and this is one that I cannot wait to see. After the Lord has washed away the filth of the people of Zion, "then [He] will create above every dwelling place of Mount Zion, and above her assemblies, a cloud and smoke by day and the shining of a flaming fire by night. For over all the glory there will be a covering" (Isaiah 4:5). The Shekinah glory of the Creator God will hover over the city of Jerusalem like a canopy—a beautiful, roiling cloud by day and an intense, powerful fire by night. Close your eyes and picture that. The Shekinah that led Israel through the wilderness will be reunited with the people once again.

Finally, the whole earth will be "full of the knowledge of the LORD as the waters cover the sea" (Isaiah 11:9). What a picture that is—the earth will know God as much as water is wet. *Wet* is the defining characteristic of water. The knowledge of God will be the defining characteristic of the earth. Is that true now? Certainly not. There are still many areas where people have never even heard of Christ. And spiritual ignorance abounds even in places where the bookstores are filled with every Bible translation you could want to have. Deception, corruption, and sin are still driving the car, while the knowledge of God has been relegated to the backseat.

From a Natural Perspective

When the millennium arrives, the world will shift politically and spiritually. And there is one other area in which we will witness momentous changes—the realm of nature.

First, the land of Israel will no longer be desolate:

> You shall also be a crown of glory in the hand of the LORD, and a royal diadem in the hand of your God. You shall no longer be termed Forsaken, nor shall your land any more be termed Desolate; but you shall be called Hephzibah, and your land Beulah; for the LORD delights in you, and your land shall be married. For as a young man marries a virgin, so shall your sons marry you; and as the bridegroom rejoices over the bride, so shall your God rejoice over you (Isaiah 62:3-5).

Hephzibah means "my delight is in her," and the name *Beulah* means "married." As you read this, you may be saying, "Wait, Amir. Hasn't God already pulled Israel out of desolation?" Yes, you are right, and extra points to you for catching that. As we read this long list of changes to expect during the millennium, this is the only one on the list that we find already completed. God has restored Israel and made it a beautiful and fertile country once again.

The second major natural difference will occur in the animal kingdom. A friend of mine tells a story of visiting the country of

Namibia to shoot video footage for a Christian ministry. While there, he and his partner went out on a safari. At one point, while my friend was taking some wonderful close-up videos of a pride of lions through an open van door, his partner yelled, "Look out!" My friend screamed and jumped to the back of the van, just waiting to feel the sensation of teeth clamping down and claws tearing flesh. Instead of hearing the roar of the attack, however, he heard laughter from the front seat, where his partner was pointing back at him with tears streaming out of his eyes.

For a brief moment, my friend had been sure that he was about to be eaten by a lion. Why? Because that's what lions do. Few of us would dare to walk up to a lion and say, "Here, kitty, kitty," and those few who did would likely do it only once. That is the nature of nature ever since the fall.

But in the millennium, the animal kingdom will be restored to its original perfection.

> The wolf also shall dwell with the lamb, the leopard shall lie down with the young goat, the calf and the young lion and the fatling together; and a little child shall lead them. The cow and the bear shall graze; their young ones shall lie down together; and the lion shall eat straw like the ox. The nursing child shall play by the cobra's hole, and the weaned child shall put his hand in the viper's den. They shall not hurt nor destroy in all My holy mountain, for the earth shall be full of the knowledge of the LORD as the waters cover the sea (Isaiah 11:6-9).

Poisonous animals will cease to be dangerous. Meat-eating animals will be herbivores. In that day, all members of the animal kingdom will live together in perfect peace with each other and with mankind. Truly, this is one aspect of the millennium that I am most intrigued with.

THE PROBLEMS WITH AMILLENNIALISM

After looking at all these changes that will take place with the arrival of the millennial kingdom, it amazes me that so many pastors around the world think this reign of Christ has already begun. There is a great deception among both Christians and Jews when it comes to this unprecedented period of time.

In the Jewish mindset, the millennial kingdom coincides with the first coming of the Messiah. This is one reason that the Jews reject Jesus. They look around and they don't see all the things that should be here when the Messiah reigns. "The Messiah was here? Then why do so many people still hate Israel?" "You say Jesus is the Messiah? Well, then He left without remembering to usher in that whole lamb and lion thing." They confuse Jesus' visitation with a permanent dwelling.

What makes Jesus' first visit unique? He came for only a short time, and His primary purpose was to address sin. The Jews missed that visit. They are still waiting for the second coming as if it's the first. The deceiver has deceived them. What we call the millennial kingdom, they call Israel's messianic period. How sad it is that they missed the Messiah's first visit, and when Jesus comes back to call His church to meet Him in the air, they will miss Him once again.

But the Jews are not the only ones who are confused about the millennium. The Catholic Church and most mainline Protestant churches are not looking forward to a millennium. Even within evangelical Christian churches, there are so many—particularly those from a Reformed background—who consider themselves amillennialists. Unfortunately, the enemy has done an excellent job of deceiving them.

Amillennialists—the *a* prefix meaning "no" in Greek—believe that Jesus is currently reigning over the world from heaven through the church. From their perspective, because Jesus is on His heavenly throne, that means that His kingdom has come. And if that is true, then we must be in the millennium. The millennial reign of Christ began at the cross, and it will continue until the second coming of Christ.

You might say, "Amir, just doing the basic math, it seems to me that two thousand years have passed since the cross, not one thousand." Excellent point. The amillennialists will say that the 1,000 years are not to be taken literally. That is simply a figure of speech meaning a really long time. Some will even point to the passage where Peter said, "Beloved, do not forget this one thing, that with the Lord one day is as a thousand years, and a thousand years as one day" (2 Peter 3:8). They'll say, "See, this shows that a thousand years doesn't really mean a thousand years." However, in the context of 2 Peter, this really is a figure of speech and is laid out as such. Peter used the number to demonstrate the extreme long-suffering nature of the Lord. When we see 1,000 years mentioned in Revelation 20, the context is a prophetic narrative. There are no comparisons made. Five times in the span of six verses at the beginning of Revelation 20, the specific time period of 1,000 years is mentioned.

The second problem with the amillennial view is that none of the characteristics of the millennial kingdom fit with what's happening in the world today, except for a restored land of Israel. For amillennialists, that list of political changes, spiritual changes, and changes that will take place in the natural world must be relegated to allegories. In other words, we have to believe that the words that we are reading in the Bible do not mean what they appear to mean. Instead, they are to be understood as describing what the millennial kingdom will be like from a spiritual perspective, and not a literal, physical one.

That's a huge problem, however, for the amillennial viewpoint because that means watering down Scripture. Once we say that one part of the Bible should not be taken literally, then it is easy to spread that approach to other parts. Certainly there are different genres of writing in the Bible. But we must be exceedingly careful that we don't spiritualize a passage that, by all indicators, should be read literally.

A LITERAL KINGDOM

The millennium will be a literal kingdom in which Christ reigns for 1,000 years from a physical throne in Jerusalem. There will literally be actual changes in the physical realm, the spiritual realm, and the natural realm. I use the word *literally* on purpose because the changes are spelled out to us in the Word of God—spoken by the prophets and witnessed by the apostle John.

Before you read on to the next chapter, I'd like you to stop for a moment. Touch your arm. Do you feel the physicality of your body? Tap your foot on the ground. Do you sense the solid mass of the floor below you? Step outside. Do you feel the breeze that may be wisping across your face and gently flowing through your hair? Do you see the genuine nature of the landscape around you? That is because you are a real person living in a real world.

This is the same reality that you will experience in the millennium. It's possible that our skin might feel a little different in our incorruptible bodies. It's likely the landscape will have changed some during the devastation of the tribulation. However, when those 1,000 years begin, you and I won't be disembodied spirits hovering in an ethereal world. We will get to experience every sight, sound, taste, and smell as we physically experience Jesus Christ's reign on this earth. Close your eyes and try to picture walking up the marble steps of a grand building, entering a vast hall, and seeing at its end your Savior sitting on His throne. Wow, what a moment that will be when it happens!

CHAPTER 12

THE MILLENNIUM—WHO'S LEFT IN THE NEIGHBORHOOD?

WE HAVE ALREADY SEEN THAT WITH THE ARRIVAL of the millennium will come great changes. But rather than all things becoming new, there are many parts of this world that will become old again. What I mean is that much of this earth will return to the original state in which God created it. There will be peace on earth. All God's creatures will dwell together in harmony. The Lord Himself will be among His people, and they will worship Him in person. The world will have a nostalgic quality to it, similar to what was once enjoyed in the Garden of Eden.

THE CONFUSION ABOUT THE MILLENNIUM

In the United States, you can find any kind of music you like on the radio—hard, soft, old, new, Christian, definitely not Christian. There is one genre of stations that play what is called classics.

But the word *classic* means different things to different people. For some, it's the rock of the seventies and eighties. For others, it's the big bands of the thirties and forties. Still others look back to previous centuries to find their classics. I remember riding in a car once with a friend when his teenage daughter piped up from the back seat, "Oh, this song is a classic. It's from like 2005." In that moment, I felt my body age ten years.

The Jewish people are excitedly anticipating the classic nature of the millennium. They can't wait for the world of Israel's heyday to come back into style. The only problem is that their definition of *classic* doesn't look back far enough. This is particularly true when it comes to the one who will be sitting on the throne in Jerusalem. The Jews are looking for a new King David—a human Messiah. However, in doing so, the Jewish people are thinking way too small. Rather than celebrating the time of Israel's monarchy, they need to be looking back to when the Lord Himself led the nation through a cloud and through fire.

This confusion is understandable. Ezekiel wrote, "I will establish one shepherd over them, and he shall feed them—My servant David. He shall feed them and be their shepherd. And I, the LORD, will be their God, and My servant David a prince among them; I, the LORD, have spoken" (34:23-24). Here, Scripture clearly states that David will be the one shepherd over the people. In Jeremiah, the Lord says, "They shall serve the LORD their God, and David their king, whom I will raise up for them" (Jeremiah 30:9). It certainly seems as if a new messianic David—or even a "raised up" David himself—is going to be the one on the throne during this 1,000-year rule.

To alleviate this confusion, we need to grasp two facts. First, we must understand that there are two resurrections, and second, we need to know how the Bible uses typology.

Understanding the Two Resurrections

In Scripture, the first resurrection begins with Jesus, who is "the firstfruits of those who have fallen asleep" (1 Corinthians 15:20). Because Christ is called the "firstfruits," we can assume that more will be resurrected later. This assumption is played out at the rapture when the church is taken to be with Christ:

> This we say to you by the word of the Lord, that we who are alive and remain until the coming of the Lord will by no means precede those who are asleep. For the Lord Himself will descend from heaven with a shout, with the voice of an archangel, and with the trumpet of God. And the dead in Christ will rise first. Then we who are alive and remain shall be caught up together with them in the clouds to meet the Lord in the air. And thus we shall always be with the Lord (1 Thessalonians 4:15-17).

All believers who have died during the church age will be resurrected at that glorious moment to be with Christ forever.

Now, the rapture does not end the first resurrection. In the middle of the tribulation, two more men will rise from the dead. For three-and-a-half years, God will use these two witnesses to preach truth from Jerusalem. People aren't going to like what they have to say, so they will try to kill them. Bad idea. "If anyone wants to harm them, fire proceeds from their mouth and devours their enemies. And if anyone wants to harm them, he must be killed in this manner" (Revelation 11:5). These two will become the most hated men on the planet—not only because they will tell people things they don't want to hear, but they will follow up their words up with plagues, drought, famine, and what sounds like the worst case of dragon breath ever recorded.

Finally, at the end of the two witnesses' mission, the beast will rise up and kill them, leaving their bodies to rot in the streets of

Jerusalem. This will lead to a worldwide party. Everyone will be so relieved to not have to hear these two that they'll fill the streets in celebration and exchange gifts with one another. Dead Witnesses' Day cards will sell out in all the grocery stores. Isn't that how it is today? People don't want to hear about their own sin. They would rather attack those who call them out for their immorality than do anything to change their unrighteous actions.

But the merrymakers' party will quickly come to an end. Three-and-a-half days later, "the breath of life from God" will enter the witnesses, and they will stand up, with great fear falling on everyone who sees this. A voice from heaven will say, "Come up here," and they will ascend "to heaven in a cloud" (Revelation 11:11-12). This resurrection will be followed by a huge earthquake that rocks Jerusalem, leveling a tenth of the city and killing 7,000 people.

After this, the first resurrection will not be over yet. At the end of Jacob's trouble—or the tribulation—all the Old Testament saints will be resurrected.

> At that time Michael shall stand up, the great prince who stands watch over the sons of your people; and there shall be a time of trouble, such as never was since there was a nation, even to that time. And at that time your people shall be delivered, every one who is found written in the book. And many of those who sleep in the dust of the earth shall awake, some to everlasting life, some to shame and everlasting contempt (Daniel 12:1-2).

Imagine the patriarchs Abraham, Isaac, and Jacob physically back on the earth. As you walk through the streets during the millennium, you may pass Moses or Elijah or Jonah (who hopefully by that time will have gotten the fish smell out of his hair). Maybe you'll attend an evening symposium at the convention center, where heroes like Noah and Samson and Esther will captivate their listeners with all the details of their harrowing experiences.

There is yet one more group of people who will have part in this first resurrection. These are the tribulation martyrs—those who become Christians during the seven years of God's wrath, then are killed for their beliefs.

> I saw thrones, and they sat on them, and judgment was committed to them. Then I saw the souls of those who had been beheaded for their witness to Jesus and for the word of God, who had not worshiped the beast or his image, and had not received his mark on their foreheads or on their hands. And they lived and reigned with Christ for a thousand years. But the rest of the dead did not live again until the thousand years were finished. This is the first resurrection. Blessed and holy is he who has part in the first resurrection. Over such the second death has no power, but they shall be priests of God and of Christ, and shall reign with Him a thousand years (Revelation 20:4-6).

The raising up of this final group leads John to close the door by saying, "This is the first resurrection."

Notice in the above passage that there is another group that will be brought back from the dead. They are "the rest of the dead"— those who will not come to life again until after the 1,000 years are finished. These resurrection stragglers are the unbelieving dead. They will be raised up to judgment:

> Then I saw a great white throne and Him who sat on it, from whose face the earth and the heaven fled away. And there was found no place for them. And I saw the dead, small and great, standing before God, and books

were opened. And another book was opened, which is the Book of Life. And the dead were judged according to their works, by the things which were written in the books. The sea gave up the dead who were in it, and Death and Hades delivered up the dead who were in them. And they were judged, each one according to his works. Then Death and Hades were cast into the lake of fire. This is the second death. And anyone not found written in the Book of Life was cast into the lake of fire (Revelation 20:11-15).

This is not a resurrection that anyone wants to be a part of. Notice that at this time every unbeliever will be resurrected. It doesn't matter what time period they are from, what part of the world they lived in, or what their beliefs were.

At some point, every single person who has ever lived will experience a resurrection. The only difference will be where people spend eternity after they have been raised up. Jesus made it clear that the only way to get to heaven and know happiness and joy in the presence of the one true God is by believing in Him. He said, "God so loved the world that He gave His only begotten Son, that whoever believes in Him should not perish but have everlasting life" (John 3:16). If you have not believed in Jesus Christ for your salvation and asked Him to be your Lord, now is the time to do it. By giving yourself to Him, heart and soul, you will ensure that you'll take part in the first resurrection, which leads to eternal life, and not the second resurrection, which leads to eternal death—a forever separated from God.

To understand the "David" passages at the beginning of this chapter, first we needed to make sense of the two resurrections. Now we will examine how the Bible uses typology, where one person or thing presages another.

Understanding How the Bible Uses Typology

Through the prophet Malachi, the Lord promised, "Behold, I will send you Elijah the prophet before the coming of the great and dreadful day of the LORD. And he will turn the hearts of the fathers to the children, and the hearts of the children to their fathers, lest I come and strike the earth with a curse" (Malachi 4:5-6). According to this prophecy, the prophet Elijah will return from his fiery ascension up into heaven to walk the earth again.

Jesus agreed with this Malachi prophecy. At the transfiguration, Peter, James, and John saw Jesus speaking with Moses and Elijah. Blown away by what they had just seen, the disciples asked Him, "Why do the scribes say that Elijah must come first?" Jesus answered, "Indeed, Elijah is coming first and restores all things. And how is it written concerning the Son of Man, that He must suffer many things and be treated with contempt? But I say to you that Elijah has also come, and they did to him whatever they wished, as it is written of him'" (Mark 9:11-13). Is this appearance with Moses what Malachi the prophet was speaking about? Not according to Jesus. He said that "they did to him whatever they wished." Yet nobody did anything to Elijah on the Mount of Transfiguration. This means Jesus must have been talking about another time.

In Matthew 11, Jesus talked about John the Baptist with the multitudes. He taught about how this messenger was both the greatest and the least in the kingdom of God. Then He said, "If you are willing to receive it, he is Elijah who is to come" (Matthew 11:14). John the Baptist is the fulfillment of that prophecy in Malachi. Elijah and his ministry were a type—or a foreshadowing—of a greater ministry that was to come, that of John the Baptist. This is identical to the way that the Passover and the Feasts served as shadows of what was to come.

This same kind of typology is found in the connection between David and Christ. The Jews sometimes referred to the Messiah as "David" because they knew that the Messiah would come from David's lineage. The New Testament also speaks of Jesus as the "Son of David." On one occasion, when Jesus was passing through Jericho, a blind man named Bartimaeus called out, "Jesus, Son of David, have mercy on me!" (Mark 10:47). Proclaiming this title was this man's way of affirming his belief that Jesus was the promised Messiah.

There are other typological connections between David and Jesus. In the Old Testament, King David was a man after God's own heart, was an unlikely king of God's own choosing, and the Spirit of God was upon him. Each of these characteristics could also be said of Jesus. Nevertheless, the eternal King who will rule from David's throne will not be David—it will be Jesus Christ.

That's not to say David will not be ruling at all. The great King David will be resurrected at the beginning of the millennium along with all the other Old Testament saints. He will be among those who will reign with Jesus in the kingdom. "Then the kingdom and dominion, and the greatness of the kingdoms under the whole heaven, shall be given to the people, the saints of the Most High. His kingdom is an everlasting kingdom, and all dominions shall serve and obey Him" (Daniel 7:27). Yet as evidenced by the word "people" in that verse, David will not be the only human ruler. All believers, past and present, will rule the nations and judge the world. The apostle Paul wrote, "Do you not know that the saints will judge the world? And if the world will be judged by you, are you unworthy to judge the smallest matters?" (1 Corinthians 6:2). We had better get our black robes ironed and our gavels polished, because those judging saints include you and me.

What does this judging look like? We don't really know. The

Lord has chosen to keep the details to Himself. It's as if He gave us a newspaper headline without revealing the rest of the story. Maybe He knew that if we had a long list of particulars we would dwell too much on the future and not enough on the present. So, in His great wisdom, He decided to let us know just enough. "To him who overcomes I will grant to sit with Me on My throne, as I also overcame and sat down with My Father on His throne," Jesus promises in Revelation 3:21. Wow, what a picture!

Based on that promise, we know that in some sense, we will share authority with Christ. And there is also evidence that our individual authority in the millennial kingdom will be based on how we handle the responsibilities God gives to us here on earth. Jesus tells the story of a nobleman who had to leave the country for a while. He called together ten of his servants and gave each of them a mina (an amount of money worth about three months' wages) to do business with while he was gone.

Upon his return home, the nobleman called his servants back together. He called the servants to report to him how they had done. "Then came the first, saying, 'Master, your mina has earned ten minas.' And he said to him, 'Well done, good servant; because you were faithful in a very little, have authority over ten cities.' And the second came, saying, 'Master, your mina has earned five minas.' Likewise he said to him, 'You also be over five cities'" (Luke 19:16-19).

All was looking good until the third man stepped forward. "I took your mina and hid it away, because I was afraid of what you would do if I lost it," he said. This infuriated the nobleman. "And he said to those who stood by, 'Take the mina from him, and give it to him who has ten minas…For I say to you, that to everyone who has will be given; and from him who does not have, even what he has will be taken away from him'" (Luke 19:24-26). The Lord is watching what you do now with what He has given to you. If you do much here in this life, He will know that He can trust you with much when you rule with Him in the millennial kingdom.

With this understanding of biblical typology, can we now answer who will sit on the global throne in Jerusalem? It will be Jesus as the King of kings. Humanly speaking, Jesus is from the Davidic dynasty. But in power, in glory, in righteousness, and in every other way, He is rightly called the Greater David, and "the government will be on his shoulders" (Isaiah 9:6).

A JERUSALEM LANDING

We've seen the *who* of the Millennial reign—Jesus, the King of kings and Lord of lords. The next questions have to do with *where*. Where will this millennial reign begin? And where will it be based?

As we've just discussed, the answers for both of those questions are one and the same—Jerusalem. This is why it was essential that Jerusalem get back into the hands of the Jewish people. This is also why it was such a momentous action when President Donald Trump moved the American embassy back to Jerusalem. Many people took this move lightly, but it was prophetically significant for the world's greatest superpower to recognize Jerusalem as the capital of Israel. This would have been unheard of during the 1,800 years after the final Jewish rebellions against Rome in the second century AD. For nearly 2,000 years, it would have been impossible for the second coming to take place and the millennium to begin. But today, beyond a shadow of a doubt, Jerusalem belongs to the Jews, and we have taken one more giant step toward the day approaching.

> Today, beyond a shadow of a doubt, Jerusalem belongs to the Jews, and we have taken one more giant step toward the day approaching.

A Jewish Jerusalem opens the door for Jesus' return at the end of the tribulation.

> Then the LORD will go forth and fight against those nations, as He fights in the day of battle. And in that day His feet will stand on the Mount of Olives, which faces Jerusalem on the east. And the Mount of Olives shall be split in two, from east to west, making a very large valley; half of the mountain shall move toward the north and half of it toward the south (Zechariah 14:3-4).

The Mount of Olives stands just east of the old city of Jerusalem. Typically, when you see panoramic pictures of the Temple Mount and the city of Jerusalem, they are taken from the Mount of Olives. If you ever come visit the Holy Land, you will no doubt stand upon this hill to take in the beautiful view.

Imagine the expression Jesus will have on His face when His foot touches down once again on the Mount of Olives. Will it be a look of triumph or sorrow? Will it be a look of love or judgment? If you belong to the Lord, you'll never know. His expression will remain a mystery to you because you'll be staring at His back. We who are the Lord's people will return with Him, but He will be leading the charge. He will be consuming His enemies with the breath of His mouth. We will be behind Him, following His lead. When we leave this earth, we will see Jesus' face. When we return, we will see His back.

With Jesus returning just outside Jerusalem's city walls, the question arises as to how the Jews will react. Will they be cheering? Will they be terrified? Will they once again be yelling "Crucify Him!" as they did so many years ago?

The Lord answers this, saying, "I will pour on the house of David and on the inhabitants of Jerusalem the Spirit of grace and supplication; then they will look on Me whom they pierced. Yes, they will mourn for Him as one mourns for his only son, and grieve for Him as one grieves for a firstborn" (Zechariah 12:10). In Hosea, He says, "I will return again to My place till they acknowledge their offense. Then they will seek My face; in their affliction they will earnestly seek Me" (Hosea 5:15). When the Lord returns, the remaining Jews will realize that they have been wrong all along. In that moment, they will recognize that Jesus is the true Messiah.

Once that recognition takes place, God will pour out His grace upon His people. When the Jews finally seek the Lord, He will be found by them. They will cry out once more, "*Baruch hashem Adonai*...Blessed is He who comes in the name of the Lord!" This is the glorious revival promised by Paul in Romans 11:26-27: "All Israel will be saved, as it is written: 'The Deliverer will come out of Zion, and He will turn away ungodliness from Jacob; for this is My covenant with them, when I take away their sins.'" Praise our faithful God, whose word remains true and whose love never fails!

Jeremiah gives us a clear view of the role the Jewish people will have during the millennium. He portrays this period as a time when Israel and Judah will be united once again in peace, and the city of Jerusalem will be called "The Throne of the LORD."

> At that time Jerusalem shall be called The Throne of the LORD, and all the nations shall be gathered to it, to the name of the LORD, to Jerusalem. No more shall they follow the dictates of their evil hearts. In those days the house of Judah shall walk with the house of Israel, and they shall come together out of the land of the north to the land that I have given as an inheritance to your fathers (Jeremiah 3:17-18).

The divided kingdom will be united once again under the banner of the Lord. Jesus, the righteous Branch, will reign as King "and prosper, and execute judgment and righteousness in the earth" (Jeremiah

23:5). And because of His new role as King, the name of Jesus will be changed to *Yahweh-Tsidkenu*, which means "the LORD our righteousness" (verse 6).

While Jesus is reigning as the King of kings, there will also be a king of the nation of Israel. "They shall serve the LORD their God, and David their king, whom I will raise up for them" (Jeremiah 30:9). Remember that David, along with all the Old Testament saints, will be raised up at the end of the tribulation. Thus, after so many years, King David will once again take his rightful seat on the throne in Israel. Under his leadership, the enemies of Israel will be destroyed (verse 11), the city of Jerusalem and the temple will be rebuilt (verse 18), and the population will be multiplied (verse 19).

No wonder "the virgin [shall] rejoice in the dance, and the young men and the old, together; for I will turn their mourning to joy, will comfort them, and make them rejoice rather than sorrow" (Jeremiah 31:13). The Lord will do as He promised, taking their hearts of stone and giving them hearts of flesh. He will enter a new covenant with them:

> I will put My law in their minds, and write it on their hearts; and I will be their God, and they shall be My people. No more shall every man teach his neighbor, and every man his brother, saying, "Know the LORD," for they all shall know Me, from the least of them to the greatest of them, says the LORD. For I will forgive their iniquity, and their sin I will remember no more (verses 33-34).

The streets of Jerusalem will once again be filled with "the voice of joy and the voice of gladness" (Jeremiah 33:11)!

What a day it will be when those divine feet touch earth once again. The resurrected church will return with her husband, and the Jewish people will recognize their Messiah. This will be a time of wrath and revival, of war and reconciliation. But once the frenzy of the second coming dies down, what then? By my count, there are resurrection-bodied church folk, resurrection-bodied Old Testament saints, normal-bodied recently believing Jews, and normal-bodied tribulation believers who have somehow survived the judgments. Just because you throw a bunch of vegetables into a bowl doesn't mean you'll end up with a salad. So how is this going to work?

CHAPTER 13

THE MILLENNIUM—MORE THAN A LONG TIME-OUT

IN THE PAST, WHEN A CHILD was getting out of control or had to be disciplined for some offense, the punishment was typically physical. While some parents went overboard into abuse, most children just experienced a swat to the backside or a slap to the back of the hand. Today, we live in a kinder, gentler time. Physical discipline is frowned upon by a vast swath of society. Instead, parents are encouraged to explain to their children why their behavior was bad and the reasons they should consider not doing it again in the future. If that doesn't work, then the offending child should be banished to time-out.

For many, the millennium appears to be a long time-out for Satan. He's been extremely naughty over the years, and God is finally fed up with him. So it's off to the corner, young man, so that you can think about what you've done and what you need to do to straighten up.

But is that really what those 1,000 years are all about?

As we wrap up our look at the millennium, there are four final issues we must address: What will Jerusalem look like during those 1,000 years? Who will be in the millennial kingdom, and how might they interact with one another? What is the purpose of the millennium? And why is it so vitally important that we study all this today?

JERUSALEM IN THE MILLENNIUM

Let's begin with Jerusalem. The Jerusalem that is in Israel today is the same Jerusalem that will be in Israel in the millennium. The New Jerusalem will not descend from the sky until God has created the new heaven and new earth (Revelation 21:1-2). However, there will be at least one fairly major structural change, and it has to do with water.

In Ezekiel 47, in the midst of a vision, the prophet is being led around the temple by a bronze-looking man who was carrying a line of flax and a measuring rod. When Ezekiel was led to the door of the temple, he noticed that water was flowing from under the threshold out toward the east. This is something new. I can tell you right now that not only is there no temple in Jerusalem, but the only water that might flow from the Temple Mount is if a pipe breaks under the al-Aqsa Mosque.

The bronzish man leads Ezekiel around until they exit the north gate of the temple, and there was the water still flowing down. The two followed along the stream five hundred yards, and they checked the depth using the old "stand-in-the-water" method. Here, the stream was ankle deep. They walked another five football fields' distance, and this time the water came up to Ezekiel's knees. Five hundred more yards, and the water was waist-deep. Five hundred more, and it became a full-on river so deep that Ezekiel had to swim to keep his head above the surface. Then the bronze man brought Ezekiel back to the shore.

> When I returned, there, along the bank of the river, were very many trees on one side and the other. Then he said to me: "This water flows toward the eastern region, goes down into the valley, and enters the sea. When it reaches the sea, its waters are healed. And it shall be that every living thing that moves, wherever the rivers go, will live. There will be a very great multitude of fish, because these waters go there; for they will be healed, and everything will live wherever the river goes. It shall be that fishermen will stand by it from En Gedi to En Eglaim; they will be places for spreading their nets. Their fish will be of the same kinds as the fish of the Great Sea, exceedingly many. But its swamps and marshes will not be healed; they will be given over to salt. Along the bank of the river, on this side and that, will grow all kinds of trees used for food; their leaves will not wither, and their fruit will not fail. They will bear fruit every month, because their water flows from the sanctuary. Their fruit will be for food, and their leaves for medicine" (Ezekiel 47:7-12).

The sea that this river heads toward is the Dead Sea, which is called the Dead Sea for a reason—it is a dead sea. The salt content is so high that nothing can live in it. However, when these future healing waters flow from the temple and make the 20-mile journey to the Dead Sea, life will come with the water. Suddenly, what has been lifeless for so long will be teeming with life. What was once empty and barren will be filled with hope and joy. What a picture that is of the living water that Jesus offered to the Samaritan woman in John 4:10-14! That which was dead in sin is washed clean and purified by the water that Jesus gives. Life comes—a life not just for today, but for eternity.

You may have caught one other detail in Ezekiel's vision. The water will flow from the threshold of the temple. For there to be a threshold, there must be a temple. From what we learned in earlier chapters, you may be saying, "Of course, Amir—that is the temple that the Antichrist allows the Jews to build." You would think so, but you would be wrong. This is the fourth temple.

The first temple was the temple of Solomon. Lavish and ornate, filled with gold and smelling of cedar, this is the temple that Jews of all ages think back to and sigh longingly for. This first temple was destroyed by the Babylonians in 586 BC.

The second temple was started by Zerubbabel in 516 BC after the return from the Babylonian exile. Later, this structure was greatly enhanced by Herod the Great in the time leading up to Jesus' birth. This temple survived until AD 70, when the Romans destroyed it along with much of the city of Jerusalem.

The tribulation temple is the third in line. It will have the shortest life span of any of the temples. Zechariah prophesied, "In that day His feet will stand on the Mount of Olives, which faces Jerusalem on the east. And the Mount of Olives shall be split in two, from east to west, making a very large valley; half of the mountain shall move toward the north and half of it toward the south" (Zechariah 14:4). This massive shift in the earth's surface will cause an earthquake that will level everything for miles and miles.

With the third temple gone, there is need for one more before temples become obsolete with the new heavens and new earth, when "the Lord God Almighty and the Lamb are its temple" (Revelation 21:22). This fourth temple will be built at the beginning of the millennium and will serve as the world's center for worship for 1,000 years. This is the temple to which all mankind will travel from all the corners of the earth, as we will soon see in Zechariah 14. Among those who will travel there to worship are the remnant who survive the great tribulation, along with their offspring, who will have been born during the 1,000-year kingdom.

WHAT WILL WE DO DURING THE MILLENNIUM?

In the coming millennial kingdom, the resurrected will have roles and activities to carry out. This will not just be 1,000 years of playing with pandas and cuddling with koalas. Our service to Christ will continue. "Blessed and holy is he who has part in the first resurrection. Over such the second death has no power, but they shall be priests of God and of Christ, and shall reign with Him a thousand years" (Revelation 20:6). In some capacity or other, we, the resurrected, will have authority and leadership as Christ's representatives.

The logical implication is that if we are the reigners, then there must be others who are the reignees. These reignees will be the tribulation survivors and their subsequent descendants. There will be believers who gave their lives to Christ during the tribulation and somehow avoided being slaughtered during the seven years of God's wrath. Alongside them will be the Jews who are part of the mass revival of Romans 11. But before either of these groups will be admitted into the millennium, they must face the judgment seat of Christ.

When Jesus comes back the second time, He will do so to judge:

> When the Son of Man comes in His glory, and all the holy angels with Him, then He will sit on the throne of His glory. All the nations will be gathered before Him, and He will separate them one from another, as a shepherd divides his sheep from the goats. And He will set the sheep on His right hand, but the goats on the left (Matthew 25:31-33).

Jesus goes on to say that He Himself will look at those sheep on His right and tell them, "You all did a fantastic job. You fed Me when I was hungry, sated my thirst, clothed Me, visited Me in My sickness, and lifted my spirits when I was a prisoner." Confused, those on His right will protest, saying, "O King, we don't remember seeing You when we were doing all that stuff." The King will reply, "Assuredly, I say to you, inasmuch as you did it to one of the least of these My brethren, you did it to Me" (Matthew 25:40). Those on His right will then be invited into the millennial kingdom.

Listening to this exchange with a growing dread will be the goats on the left. Sure enough, when King Jesus turns to them, He will say, "Away with you. All those things that I just said that the sheep did, you didn't do." The goats will protest, "Lord, when did we see You hungry or thirsty or a stranger or naked or sick or in prison, and did not minister to You?" (Matthew 25:44). Jesus will say that by neglecting the "least of these" they had neglected Him, and He will conclude with the pronouncement, "These will go away into everlasting punishment, but the righteous into eternal life" (Matthew 25:46).

When the sheep enter the millennium, they will still have their earthly bodies. This means that they will be able to multiply. It may seem that the reigner-to-reignee ratio may initially be skewed to the former, given the devastation of the tribulation versus the millions reconciled to Christ over the years. Over time, that number disparity will likely flip. The world population estimates for the year AD 1000 are anywhere from 250 million to 350 million. Now the estimate is around 7.5 billion. That is in an imperfect world where life expectancies are in the mid to upper two digits, depending on location and era.

But in the millennial era, life expectancies will mirror those of the early period of creation—the time prior to sin's increasingly devastating impact upon humanity and the world. It won't be unusual for many generations of a family line to all be alive at the same time. You may meet a young man on the road and say, "Hey, I recognize you. You have your great-great-great-great-great-great-grandfather's eyes…and temper."

Sin will still exist in the millennium, thus death will also remain. While people will live longer, they will still die. Those of us in our glorified bodies, however, will not. Remember, we will have been changed.

> Behold, I tell you a mystery: We shall not all sleep, but we shall all be changed—in a moment, in the twinkling of an eye, at the last trumpet. For the trumpet will sound, and the dead will be raised incorruptible, and we shall be changed. For this corruptible must put on incorruption, and this mortal must put on immortality. So when this corruptible has put on incorruption, and this mortal has put on immortality, then shall be brought to pass the saying that is written: "Death is swallowed up in victory" (1 Corinthians 15:51-54).

When the rapture takes place, our bodies will get the ultimate upgrade. We'll trade in the old, clunker minivan for a sleek, new sports car. And the wonderful thing is, this sports car will never break down or get a dent—you won't even have to buy the extended warranty. Think about it: When you get that twinkle-of-an-eye body swap, you will never again have to worry about what you eat. You can have as many donuts as you like and never gain weight. The reignees, who are still susceptible to all the negatives of the old flesh, will only be able to eat one donut before having to jog three miles to work off the calories. You and your friends, however, can hang out at the donut shop and take advantage of the "Buy six dozen, get six dozen free" sale. That fact alone is reason enough to believe!

The millennium will be a time of immortals interacting with

mortals. The sinless will be around the still sinful. Incorruptible flesh will live alongside corruptible flesh. It will be a time when all humanity—no matter their bodily status—will gather together to worship King Jesus on His throne.

> It shall come to pass that everyone who is left of all the nations which came against Jerusalem shall go up from year to year to worship the King, the LORD of hosts, and to keep the Feast of Tabernacles. And it shall be that whichever of the families of the earth do not come up to Jerusalem to worship the King, the LORD of hosts, on them there will be no rain. If the family of Egypt will not come up and enter in, they shall have no rain; they shall receive the plague with which the LORD strikes the nations who do not come up to keep the Feast of Tabernacles. This shall be the punishment of Egypt and the punishment of all the nations that do not come up to keep the Feast of Tabernacles (Zechariah 14:16-19).

Zechariah's prophecy starts out so well, and if it ended after the first sentence, then all would be great. Sadly, it does not. Sin is sin, flesh is flesh, and humanity is humanity. Even with Jesus physically on the throne in Jerusalem and the devil in the bottomless pit, people will still rebel against God. It is here that we come to the purpose of the millennium.

WHY DO WE EVEN NEED A MILLENNIUM?

One reason some people have difficulty believing in a literal, physical, earthly 1,000-year reign of Christ is that they don't see the reason for it. Isn't it kind of a random event? History travels along with relative normalcy until all of a sudden there is this strange and extremely long parenthetical period. Is God just taking an extended vacation? Again, as we noted earlier, is this actually a disciplinary time-out for Satan to see if he can finally get his act together and apologize for his naughty behavior?

This really isn't as much of a mystery as some people make it out to be. Rather than the millennium's purpose being elusive, for many Christians, it's just uncomfortable. What was the reason for Jesus' first coming? "God did not send His Son into the world to condemn the world, but that the world through Him might be saved" (John 3:17). This is how most of us prefer to see Jesus—the loving, sacrificial Savior. It fits so much better

> In the peace and beauty of the millennium, no one will be able to miss the evidences of God's character.

with the sweet, cuddly baby Jesus whom we put on display at Christmas. We like the 70 x 7 forgiveness of our gentle and merciful Lord.

This is why the second coming of Christ shakes up so many. When Jesus returns, He will do so not with a hug, but a sword. Paul told the Athenians, "Truly, these times of ignorance God overlooked, but now commands all men everywhere to repent, because He has appointed a day on which He will judge the world in righteousness by the Man whom He has ordained. He has given assurance of this to all by raising Him from the dead" (Acts 17:30-31). When Jesus returns, it will not be as Savior, but as Judge.

Notice the qualifier that describes the kind of judgment Christ will bring. When He judges, it will be "in righteousness." If God is going to judge the world on this basis, He will want to make sure that His righteousness has been clearly on display (Isaiah 11; 61). The truth was preached at His first coming, and will be displayed at His second coming. In the peace and beauty of the millennium, no one will be able to miss the evidences of God's character. It will be on exhibit in nature and amongst the nations.

Maybe you missed Jesus in His first coming; maybe He wasn't quite what you were looking for. Now, here He is again. Jesus is reigning from Jerusalem. Satan is not around to deceive or distract. In such conditions, it seems that everyone would automatically believe. But they won't.

Remarkably, in spite of all the righteous confirmation around them, masses of millennial mortals will still turn their backs on the Savior. It is here we find a second millennial purpose that offsets the display of God's righteousness. Where there is sin and rebellion, there must be judgment.

Two judgments will take place in the millennial kingdom. The first we've already looked at—the sheep and the goats mentioned in Matthew 25. This is the same judgment that the prophet Joel wrote about:

> Behold, in those days and at that time,
> when I bring back the captives of Judah and Jerusalem,
> I will also gather all nations,
> and bring them down to the Valley of Jehoshaphat;
> and I will enter into judgment with them there
> on account of My people, My heritage Israel (Joel 3:1-2).

It is from the sheep of this judgment—the newly saved Jews and the surviving tribulation believers—that the millennial kingdom will be populated. But, as we've already seen, the spiritual perfection of that first generation of millennials won't last. Thus, when Satan is finally released, he will find a ready-made army eager for him to lead them in a military rebellion against the Lord. This is the second and greater battle of Gog and Magog spoken of in the Bible:

> When the thousand years have expired, Satan will be
> released from his prison and will go out to deceive the
> nations which are in the four corners of the earth, Gog

and Magog, to gather them together to battle, whose number is as the sand of the sea. They went up on the breadth of the earth and surrounded the camp of the saints and the beloved city. And fire came down from God out of heaven and devoured them (Revelation 20:7-9).

When the Lord accomplishes His sure victory in that battle, the end will have come for all sin, rebellion, and death. Satan will then be cast into the lake of fire to join the beast and the false prophet, who met that fate 1,000 years earlier.

This is when the second of the millennial judgments, the Great White Throne judgment, will occur. Jesus, in all His godly glory, will sit before all the people of the world who will have gathered before Him:

> I saw a great white throne and Him who sat on it, from whose face the earth and the heaven fled away. And there was found no place for them. And I saw the dead, small and great, standing before God, and books were opened. And another book was opened, which is the Book of Life. And the dead were judged according to their works, by the things which were written in the books. The sea gave up the dead who were in it, and Death and Hades delivered up the dead who were in them. And they were judged, each one according to his works. Then Death and Hades were cast into the lake of fire. This is the second death. And anyone not found written in the Book of Life was cast into the lake of fire (Revelation 20:11-15).

This will be a somber and tragic day. At this point, all those who have rejected God, from Cain through to the end, will stand before this judicial King. They will finally understand the depths of their rebellion. They'll recognize the heinous nature of their sins. They will realize the righteousness of the Lord's justice as it is meted out to them. And they will wail in sorrow as they are cast into the lake of fire for all eternity.

It is painful to even write about this. People I know—people I love—will face the Lord at this judgment. I can close my eyes and picture the terrified and remorseful looks on their faces as they hear the verdict pronounced. I can't bring myself to take that next step of visualizing them cast to their just punishment. Friend, let this be a motivator for you to strive to live and speak the gospel to all those around you. Even if people reject or mock you because of your boldness, isn't that a small price to pay for the chance that you might play a part in rescuing them from this final judgment?

The time is short. We must be about our Father's business.

WHY DO WE NEED TO STUDY THE MILLENNIUM?

"Amir," you may say, "all this about the millennium is interesting, but is it really important? Sure, it's fun to talk about lions and lambs, but are there any essential and applicable doctrines we need to know?" Well, if the millennium is not important, then why did John have that long revelation that is recorded for us at the end of our Bibles? What about all those Old Testament prophets who had dreams and visions that provide us with details about the millennium? The very fact that God felt it was important to allocate such a significant chunk of His Word to this 1,000-year span of time should be enough to tell you that it is worth studying.

Stirring up our motivation to reach out to our loved ones is reason enough to study about the millennium. We need to know what is waiting for them if they don't open their hearts to the Savior.

Yet another purpose for pursuing what Scripture says about the millennium is that you need to ensure that you, too, are right with

God. Your decisions today will affect your place and role in the millennial kingdom. If you choose Jesus now, you will reign with Him in the future. But if you deny Him now, He will deny you before the Father. There are no promotions in the millennial kingdom. Either you will reign, or you will be reigned over. Follow Jesus today, and you will reign with Him tomorrow. Reject Jesus today, and you may not even see tomorrow. Paul wrote to Timothy, "If we died with Him, we shall also live with Him; if we endure, we shall also reign with Him. If we deny Him, He also will deny us" (2 Timothy 2:11-12). I would much rather be among the reigners than the disowned.

Make your decision now. The Bible tells us that procrastination is not an option. "Behold, now is the accepted time; behold, now is the day of salvation" (2 Corinthians 6:2). Give your heart to Christ, and you will be assured a place in the family of God, a membership into the bride of Christ, a ruling role in the millennial kingdom, and an eternity to experience our Creator's new heaven and new earth.

CHAPTER 14

A LOOK AT THE BOOKS

WE ARE FINALLY AT THE END OF TIME. It's been a long journey that we've taken—starting way back in Genesis and arriving now at the grand finale of God's magnificent symphony of history. The old is about to give way to the new; the corrupted original is ready to be set aside so that the upgraded model can take its place. Heaven and Earth 2.0 are about to be revealed. But before we can take our final steps into eternity, there is some unfinished business. There are a few events that must take place, and sin must finally be dealt with once and for all.

Prior to the millennium, the beast and his prophet were cast into the lake of fire. "The beast was captured, and with him the false prophet who worked signs in his presence, by which he deceived those who received the mark of the beast and those who worshiped his image. These two were cast alive into the lake of fire burning with brimstone" (Revelation 19:20). Later, after the rebellion at the end of the 1,000 years, Satan was also done away with for good. "The devil, who deceived them, was cast into the lake of fire and brimstone where the beast and the false prophet are. And they will be tormented day and night forever and ever" (Revelation 20:10). Good-bye. Good riddance. You will not be missed. But sin won't disappear with the removal of these three. The chiefs of sin will be gone, but the sinful will still linger.

If God's new heaven and earth are going to be perfect environments, then sin and the sinful must be dealt with. Enter the final judgment—the heavenly judicial proceeding at which people's final eternal destinies will be pronounced. Those still living with the taint of sin will be cast away once and for all, following the fate of their master, the devil. Those who have been made right with God through the blood of Jesus Christ will be saved from that terrible destiny. But how will we know who is who? It's all in the books.

THE GREAT DATA COLLECTOR

We all like our privacy. None of us want Big Brother looking over our shoulders or intervening in our lives. We cringe when we hear about Facebook and Google accumulating and storing personal information about us, and we feel betrayed when we learn that they've sold the details of our lives to data collectors and marketers. Sometimes it seems that if we even *think* about wanting to buy a new watch, there are suddenly advertisements for watches on every web page we open.

As good as Facebook and Google are at gathering specifics about us, there is One who is better. Our God is the great Data Collector. He can scrape up every scrap of information about who we are and what we do, and file all of it in the bottomless depths of His omniscient internal storage. His knowledge about us doesn't simply extend to who we are or what we've done. It also includes everything that we are ever going to do or think. How many times in the Gospels did Jesus sit with a group of people, and, knowing their thoughts ahead of time, answer their questions even before they asked them?

If we were to open the file cabinets of God's unlimited mind, what knowledge about us might we find there? Let's create a sample list:

The Works of All People

"I saw the dead, small and great, standing before God, and books were opened. And another book was opened, which is the Book of Life. And the dead were judged according to their works, by the things which were written in the books" (Revelation 20:12). God has seen every action of every person throughout all time, and He has written them in his books. There will come a day when those books will be opened and read before all mankind.

The Names of All Christians

"Anyone not found written in the Book of Life was cast into the lake of fire" (Revelation 20:15). If everyone whose name is not in the Book of Life is condemned, then to whom do the names belong which are written in the Book of Life? These are those who are not condemned—those who have given their lives to Christ and have committed to following Him day by day.

The Number and Names of All the Stars

"He counts the number of the stars; He calls them all by name" (Psalm 147:4). Okay, maybe this one isn't directly about humanity, but it's still pretty amazing. Have you ever been away from the city lights and looked up into the heavens? The view that we have

> If God cares so much about the little things, imagine His passion for the big things.

with just our naked eyes is astounding. When we realize that we are glimpsing only a tiny fraction of the universe, we are reminded of just how huge our God is. Why would God take the time to learn the names of all the stars? Actually, He didn't. He already knew them because He made them. He named each one as He created it and placed it in its perfect place—"You'll be Bob Star. You'll be Sally Star. And you—the extra sparkly one—you'll be Starry McStarster."

The Hairs on Our Heads

"The very hairs of your head are all numbered" (Matthew 10:30). Admittedly, some people's heads are less of a challenge to God than others. It's amazing that the Lord knows us so well that even a detail this seemingly meaningless is not beyond His care. If God cares so much about the little things, imagine His passion for the big things.

All Our Tears

"You number my wanderings; put my tears into Your bottle; are they not in Your book?" (Psalm 56:8). If you ever feel alone when you are crying, know that you are not. In those heartbroken times of grief and sorrow, the Lord is there feeling every tear you cry. He knows every reason that you weep.

The Physical Features of Every Person

"Your eyes saw my substance, being yet unformed. And in Your book they all were written, the days fashioned for me, when as yet there were none of them" (Psalm 139:16). At the moment of conception, God knew what you would look like. Even before He watched that first cell division, then the next split, then the next and the next—God had seen your face and took joy in the beauty of His creation.

Every Spoken Word

"I say to you that for every idle word men may speak, they will give account of it in the day of judgment" (Matthew 12:36). Remember when you said such-and-such to that person? So does God. From the shouted insults to the curses muttered under your breath, God hears them all and will hold us to account. He also hears and loves every whispered prayer and exclamation of praise—sounds that please His ears and bring joy to His heart.

> There is nothing done for the glory of God that He doesn't see and remember.

Every Godly Work

"God is not unjust to forget your work and labor of love which you have shown toward His name, in that you have ministered to the saints, and do minister" (Hebrews 6:10). When you leave a box of food on the doorstep of a family in need, God sees it. During the late nights spent cleaning the church in preparation for the next day's services, the Lord is watching. When you are shuffling along because your knees are stiff and tender from hours spent in private prayer, the Spirit has been with you every moment. There is nothing done for the glory of God that He doesn't see and remember.

Investments Made in God's Kingdom

"Do not lay up for yourselves treasures on earth, where moth and rust destroy and where thieves break in and steal; but lay up for yourselves treasures in heaven, where neither moth nor rust destroys and where thieves do not break in and steal" (Matthew 6:20-21).

I have been in many churches and participated in countless services. There are some churches where I sit down in the front row until I am called up to speak. In others, I have a chair set up for me on the stage. From that vantage point, it's amazing what I can see—often things that you think nobody sees.

I can spot those of you who are dozing, and I can see your reaction when your wife elbows you awake. I can usually tell the difference between someone looking up a Bible passage on their phone and someone checking their Facebook page while trying to make it seem as if they are looking up a Bible passage. I can also see those who, during the offering, are looking around wanting to make sure that everyone sees what they are putting into the plate. Then there are those who covertly slip something into the offering, hoping that nobody notices what they are doing. That second way is how we should give. Fold your check before you slip it into the plate. Wrap your $20 bill inside a $1 bill. God knows what we give—there's no reason anyone else ever should. We are laying up treasures in heaven, not accolades on earth.

Those Who Fear God

"Those who feared the LORD spoke to one another, and the LORD listened and heard them; so a book of remembrance was written before Him for those who fear the LORD and who meditate on His name" (Malachi 3:16). Those who worship the Lord and desire to know Him are recognized and heard by Him. He also ensures that their names are listed in His book of remembrance.

This brings us back to the books in Revelation 20:11-15. These books are filled with names and information. The first volume keeps track of all people over all time everywhere. Every person who has ever been born has been listed in this book. The second is the Book of Life. This is the list of all those who are destined to spend eternity with God.

In a sense, both books are books of life—one includes everyone who has ever been alive, and one lists everyone who will enter eternity. The former is the lesser of the books, and the latter is the greater. Like the feasts, there is the shadow, and there is the substance.

THE DUALITY OF THE BOOKS

In the two books is a kind of duality that is seen throughout Scripture. Duality is seen in our two births. How many of you reading this book were at some time in your life born? I'm betting that the percentage is fairly high. I may be going out on a limb here, but I can guarantee you that there is not one person alive on this earth who did not start out their life being born. Jesus tells us that there is another birth, however—a birth that doesn't begin your physical life, but your eternal life.

> Jesus answered and said to him, "Most assuredly, I say to you, unless one is born again, he cannot see the kingdom of God."
>
> Nicodemus said to Him, "How can a man be born when he is old? Can he enter a second time into his mother's womb and be born?"
>
> Jesus answered, "Most assuredly, I say to you, unless one is born of water and the Spirit, he cannot enter the kingdom of God" (John 3:3-5).

The first time I went to the Philippines back in 1998, before one of the services, someone approached me and asked me if I was Catholic or born again. I wasn't sure how to respond, because I know that the two are not necessarily mutually exclusive. As the evening progressed, I came to understand that "born again" is simply the term that congregation used to differentiate evangelical Christians from Catholics. Jesus' use of the phrase, however, involves more than just a title or a descriptive term. It is an amazing word picture.

The Pharisee Nicodemus couldn't figure out what Jesus meant by being born again. Isn't it impossible to return to the womb of one's mother? And, even if it wasn't, who would want to do it? Jesus explained that a person needs to be born of water and of the Spirit. Everyone is born of water. For nine months, each one of us was a great swimmer. Then the water broke, and we came out. This brought us forth to physical life.

For eternal life, we need to be born of the Spirit. The first birth—of water—is necessary for admission into the natural world. The second is necessary for admission into the heavenly world. Water birth takes place at the beginning of our time on earth. Spiritual birth can happen at any time that we still have breath. Physical birth is passive—we don't do anything to make it happen. Spiritual birth is active—it comes when we choose to follow Jesus Christ.

A second duality is seen in our two lives. Paul wrote, "If the Spirit of Him who raised Jesus from the dead dwells in you, He who raised Christ from the dead will also give life to your mortal bodies through His Spirit who dwells in you" (Romans 8:11). As we hopefully can agree, each of us is physically alive. However, the life you live now is not enough. This is simply the life of a person with a mortal body. When you are born again, then the Spirit of Him who raised Jesus from the dead will dwell in you. That is new life. The first life is temporal—it will end. The new life is eternal—it will last forever.

Similar to there being two lives, there are also two deaths. As tragic as it is, people die. "It is appointed for men to die once, but after this the judgment" (Hebrews 9:27). Death simply happens in the course of life. The physical body has an expiration date on it, and one day its time will run out. It is possible, however, to be dead even though physically we are still alive. "And you, being dead in your trespasses and the uncircumcision of your flesh, He has made alive together with Him, having forgiven you all trespasses" (Colossians 2:13). Sin kills us spiritually. But through Christ's work on the cross and the forgiveness that results, God can bring us back to life.

As we learned earlier, there are two resurrections. The first began with Jesus as "the firstfruits of those who have fallen asleep" (1 Corinthians 15:20). Lazarus died, was resurrected, then died again. No one besides Jesus ever died, resurrected, then never died again. Since He is the firstfruits, we know that when we are resurrected to be with the Lord, we, like Him, will be done with death once and for all. This first resurrection begins with Jesus and carries through to the second coming. The second resurrection will take place at the end of the millennial kingdom. Everyone who has ever lived will be part of one of these two resurrections. What your resurrection looks like will depend on another duality—whether you are a believer or an unbeliever.

This leads us to the last of the dualities—the two books. The first set of books is the lesser. They contain the names of every person ever born. The second is the Lamb's Book of Life. This is the book that ups the game from physical life to eternal life.

THE OPENING OF THE BOOKS

In Revelation 20:12, John the Revelator describes for us what will take place in heaven:

> I saw the dead, small and great, standing before God, and books were opened. And another book was opened, which is the Book of Life. And the dead were judged according to their works, by the things which were written in the books.

Imagine this amazing scene. We will all be standing before God. The books will be opened, and one by one, men and women from all generations will be judged based on their actions during their lives. Daniel is even more picturesque in his description of this same courtroom:

> I watched till thrones were put in place,
> and the Ancient of Days was seated;
> His garment was white as snow,
> and the hair of His head was like pure wool.
> His throne was a fiery flame,
> its wheels a burning fire;
> a fiery stream issued
> and came forth from before Him.
> A thousand thousands ministered to Him;
> ten thousand times ten thousand stood before Him.
> The court was seated,
> and the books were opened (Daniel 7:9-10).

This is a public trial, and all who are there will hear the sins of each defendant. With God, everything is in the open. There is nothing left hidden. Every action with its shame and guilt will be laid bare. Then will come the verdict: "Guilty!" This is a scene that makes me shudder and fills me with sorrow. However, it does not fill me with fear because I will not be judged in this courtroom. I will be in the gallery—an observer, not a defendant.

At the front of the courtroom, the books will be opened, and everyone will receive the just punishment for their own sins. Watching this from the gallery is likely to be a very difficult experience. You may see people there whom you love, people who you want to help, people who you want to rescue. But it will be too late. There will be nothing left that you can do.

You may want to stand in for someone else's sins. Moses tried that, but it didn't work. After spending time with God on Mount Sinai, he came down and saw that horrific golden calf. Forty days he was on that mountain—the presence of God with him, burning the mountain, etching out His law. Now, Moses was furious and devastated by what he saw. He knew the enormity of the people's sin and the punishment that they deserved.

Yet despite their sinfulness and rebellion against God and against him, Moses still loved these people. In fact, he loved them enough to put his eternal destiny on the line. He pleaded with the Lord, "Oh, these people have committed a great sin, and have made for themselves a god of gold! Yet now, if You will forgive their sin—but if not, I pray, blot me out of Your book which You have written" (Exodus 32:31-32). Moses was willing to have his name erased out of the Lamb's Book of Life if it would mean that the names of the Israelites remained.

But God was having none of it. He replied, "Whoever has sinned against Me, I will blot him out of My book...Nevertheless, in the day when I visit for punishment, I will visit punishment upon them for their sin" (verses 33-34). Each person will be punished for his or her own sins. There is only One substitute for our sins, and neither Moses nor we qualify.

While watching the judgment, in desperation you may want to replace your name in the Book of Life with a loved one's. Like Moses, Paul's heart broke for his people. He knew their lost condition because of their rejection of the Messiah who had been sent to them. Paul was an orthodox Jew—he understood his fellow Jews' adherence to the law, their commitment to ritual, their pride in being God's chosen people. He pleaded before God in a gut-wrenching prayer, "I could wish that I myself were accursed from Christ for my brethren, my countrymen according to the flesh" (Romans 9:3). He was saying that if his spiritual death could mean the salvation of his fellow Jews, he would assent to it in a heartbeat. But God doesn't work that way. Everyone is responsible for their own disposition in the book of judgment.

THE LAMB'S BOOK OF LIFE

It is upon this second book, the Lamb's Book of Life, that we need to place our focus and our hope. Again, the first set of books contains every name of every person ever born. The names in that book are temporary and are erased as people die. Not so with the greater book. When a name is written there, it remains.

Yom Kippur is the Jewish Day of Atonement. Leading up to that holy day, Jews fast for 25 hours. The religious requirement is a 24-hour fast, but we figure we better add an hour just to be safe. There's no telling how furious God would be if we shorted Him a minute or two. At Yom Kippur, there is a traditional blessing that we say to one another: "May your name be written in the book." This is the Book of Life or the Book of Remembrance spoken of in Malachi:

> Those who feared the LORD spoke to one another,
> and the Lord listened and heard them;
> so a book of remembrance was written before Him
> for those who fear the LORD
> and who meditate on His name.

> "They shall be Mine," says the LORD of hosts,
> "on the day that I make them My jewels.
> And I will spare them as a man spares his own son who
> serves him" (Malachi 3:16-17).

Think of how tragic this blessing is. Essentially, it is saying, "Your name may have been written in the book last year, but because you were likely so terrible this past year it's possible that your name has been erased. Here's hoping that you can make it back in."

The Jewish people understand that when it comes to the regular book of life, sin can bring death, and death removes your name from that book. However, it is different in the Lamb's Book of Life. In the first set of books, the names are written in ink. In the second and greater book, the names are written in blood. And that blood is not our own—it is the blood of the perfect Lamb of God, who shed His own blood for the remission of our sins. It is this blood that has redeemed us for eternal life. This blood is permanent, indestructible, unable to be erased. The question we need to ask is not "Can I lose my salvation?," but "Am I saved to begin with?"

IS YOUR NAME WRITTEN IN THE BOOK OF LIFE?

This brings us to the final and most important question of this entire book: Is your name written in the Book of Life? Jesus made very clear the path to salvation when He said, "I am the way, the truth, and the life. No one comes to the Father except through Me" (John 14:6).

Salvation doesn't come through a specific denomination, or from being good enough. You can't be born a Christian because your parents are Christians, and you can't have salvation poured upon your head by a pastor or a priest when you are a child. Salvation comes when you decide to give your life to Jesus, accept His free gift of salvation, and commit to living for Him.

Paul wrote, "By grace you have been saved through faith, and that not of yourselves; it is the gift of God, not of works, lest anyone should boast" (Ephesians 2:8-9). Salvation is a *God* work, not an *us* work. It is you and me accepting the Lord's invitation of grace, not us earning our way in.

How do we receive this free gift of salvation? By believing that Jesus' work on the cross is sufficient for our forgiveness and eternal life, and by committing to making Him the center of our life. "If you confess with your mouth the Lord Jesus and believe in your heart that God has raised Him from the dead, you will be saved. For with the heart one believes unto righteousness, and with the mouth confession is made unto salvation" (Romans 10:9-10). A simple prayer of faith and commitment coming from your heart is all God requires.

When you make this commitment, your relationship with Christ is restored. You are now in Him, and He is in you. It is this relationship that ensures your name is in that Book of Life. John wrote,

> This is the testimony: that God has given us eternal life, and this life is in His Son. He who has the Son has life; he who does not have the Son of God does not have life. These things I have written to you who believe in the name of the Son of God, that you may know that you have eternal life, and that you may continue to believe in the name of the Son of God (1 John 5:11-13).

Until that Day comes...let us be about our Father's business, knowing that our time is short.

Notice that word "know." How powerful and comforting it is! John does not say that you will "wish" that you have eternal life, or "hope" that you have eternal life. He says that you will *know* without a shadow of a doubt that your name is written in the Lamb's Book of Life, and that you will spend eternity in the new heaven and on the new earth enjoying the presence of your Savior and Lord, Jesus Christ.

ANY DAY NOW

The Day is approaching. This is the Day when Jesus will rapture His church from the earth to meet Him. This is the Day of the Lord's judgment on sinners and the discipline of His people, Israel. This is the Day when Jesus will set foot upon the Mount of Olives, coming a second time to dwell on earth with His creation. This is the Day of the rule of the King of kings from His throne in Jerusalem. This is the Day of Satan's confinement, and of his eventual release and mankind's final rebellion. This is the Day of the Great White Throne judgment, when the sheep and the goats will be separated. And it is the Day of the new heaven and new earth, where we will enjoy the presence of the Lord forever.

Until that Day comes, let us rest in the hope of salvation through Jesus Christ. And let us be about our Father's business, knowing that our time is short. As Hebrews 10:23-25 says,

> Let us hold fast the confession of our hope without wavering, for He who promised is faithful. And let us consider one another in order to stir up love and good works, not forsaking the assembling of ourselves together, as is the manner of some, but exhorting one another, and so much the more as you see the Day approaching.

NOTES

CHAPTER 1—ANY DAY NOW

1. Brooke Seipel, "Google Searches Spike for 'World War 3' amid Heightened Tensions Abroad," *The Hill*, April 14, 2017, https://thehill.com/blogs/blog-briefing-room/news/328948-google-searches-spike-for-world-war-3-amid-heightened-tensions.

2. Neil Connor and David Millward "World 'on the Brink of Thermo-Nuclear War', as North Korea Mulls Test That Could Goad Trump," *The Telegraph*, April 14, 2017, www.telegraph.co.uk/news/2017/04/13/us-may-launch-strike-north-korea-goes-nuclear-weapons-test/.

3. Dahlia Kholaif and Tamera El-Ghobashy, "Blasts Hit Two Egyptian Churches, Killing at Least 47," *The Wall Street Journal*, April 9, 2017, www.wsj.com/articles/egyptian-church-hit-by-bomb-blast-1491727099.

4. James Macintyre, "Egyptian Coptic Priest Delivers Inspiring Christian Message to Bombers: 'Thank You, We Are Praying for You,'" *Christian News on Christian Today*, April 13, 2017, www.christiantoday.com/article/egyptian-coptic-priest-delivers-inspiring-christian-message-to-bombers-thank-you-we-are-praying-for-you/107295.htm.

5. Avi Lewis, "Saudis 'Would Let Israeli Jets Use Their Air Space to Attack Iran,'" *The Times of Israel*, February 25, 2015, www.timesofisrael.com/saudis-said-to-mull-air-passage-for-israeli-jets-to-attack-iran/.

6. "List of Large Volcanic Eruptions in the 21st Century," Wikipedia, Wikimedia Foundation, May 9, 2019, https://en.wikipedia.org/wiki/List_of_large_volcanic_eruptions_in_the_21st_century.

7. "UN Issues Urgent Appeal for $4.4 Billion in Famine Aid," *Philanthropy News Digest*, March 14, 2017, http://philanthropynewsdigest.org/news/un-issues-urgent-appeal-for-4.4-billion-in-famine-aid.

CHAPTER 4—AN EXTENDED 70 WEEKS

1. *BibleGateway*. Bible Gateway Blog, www.biblegateway.com/resources/encyclopedia-of-the-bible/Apocalyptic-Literature.

2. Clarence Larkin, "Mountain Peaks of Prophecy by Clarence Larkin," http://clarencelarkincharts.com/Clarence_Larkin_6.html.

CHAPTER 5—THE LONG SHADOW OF THE PASSOVER

1. Sam Behrens, "How Creepy Holographic Concerts Are Transforming the Future of the Music Business," *Mic*, October 26, 2015, https://mic.com/articles/89785/how-creepy-holographic-concerts-are-transforming-the-future-of-the-music-business#.qPABqRxKR.

2. Ben Sales, "Christians Who Celebrate Rosh Hashanah and Yom Kippur a Growing Trend," *The Times of Israel*, August 26, 2017, www.timesofisrael.com/christians-who-celebrate-rosh-hashanah-and-yom-kippur-a-growing-trend/.

CHAPTER 6—THE LONG SHADOW OF THE OTHER FEASTS

1. "The Omer Offering," *The Temple Institute*, www.templeinstitute.org/the_omer_offering.htm.

2. Strong's Hebrew: 6016, עֹמֶר *(Omer)—Omer*, https://biblehub.com/hebrew/6016.htm.

3. Shemot Rabbah 5:9, www.sefaria.org/Shemot_Rabbah.5.9?lang=bi.

CHAPTER 7—THE VIEW FROM THE MIDDLE EAST

1. "Runaway Train Stopped After Uncontrolled 2 Hours" *CNN*, May 16, 2001, www.cnn .com/2001/US/05/15/runaway.train.05/.

2. "Demographics of Islam," Berkley Center for Religion, Peace and World Affairs, http://berk leycenter.georgetown.edu/essays/demographics-of-islam.

3. Alastair Tancred, "Saudi Arabia Offers to Build the 'Biggest' Football Stadium in Iraq," *Daily Mail Online*, Mar 13, 2018, www.dailymail.co.uk/news/article-5483295/Saudi-Arabia-offers -build-biggest-football-stadium-Iraq.html.

4. Lisa Barrington et al., "Lebanon's Hariri Rescinds Resignation, Drawing Line under Crisis," *Reuters*, December 5, 2017, www.reuters.com/article/us-lebanon-politics-idUSKBN1DZ1CG.

CHAPTER 8—THE VIEW FROM ISRAEL

1. Will Kenton, "Silicon Valley," *Investopedia*, June 25, 2018, www.investopedia.com/terms/s/sil iconvalley.asp.

2. Ed Zwirn, "Israel's Tech Startups Are Giving Silicon Valley a Run for Its Money," *New York Post*, May 28, 2017, https://nypost.com/2017/05/28/israels-tech-startups-are-giving-silicon -valley-a-run-for-its-money/.

3. Sharon Udasin, "A Drip Revolution Around the World," *The Jerusalem Post*, April 23, 2015, www.jpost.com/Israel-News/A-drip-revolution-around-the-world-398660.

4. Emily Harris, "Israel Bets on Recycled Water to Meet Its Growing Thirst," *NPR*, June 21, 2015, www.npr.org/sections/parallels/2015/06/21/415795367/israel-bets-on-recycled-water-to -meet-its-growing-thirst.

5. "Israel GDP per Capita [1960–2019] [Data & Charts]," www.ceicdata.com/en/indicator/israel/ gdp-per-capita.

6. Larisa Brown, "Migrants Wait in Libya to Cross the Sea after Italy Turned Boats Away," *Daily Mail Online*, July 9, 2018, www.dailymail.co.uk/news/article-5932107/Migrants-wait-Libya -cross-Mediterranean-Europe-Italy-turned-boats-away.html.

7. "Read the Full Jewish Nation-State Law," *The Jerusalem Post*, July 19, 2018, www.jpost.com/ Israel-News/Read-the-full-Jewish-Nation-State-Law-562923.

8. Peter Beaumont, "EU Leads Criticism After Israel Passes Jewish 'Nation State' Law," *The Guardian*, July 19, 2018, www.theguardian.com/world/2018/jul/19/israel-adopts-contro versial-jewish-nation-state-law.

9. Matt Egan, "America Is Set to Surpass Saudi Arabia in a 'Remarkable' Oil Milestone," *CNN*, March 21, 2019, www.cnn.com/2019/03/08/business/us-oil-exports-saudi-arabia/index.html.

10. "Text: Obama's Speech in Cairo," *The New York Times*, June 4, 2009, www.nytimes.com/ 2009/06/04/us/politics/04obama.text.html.

11. Habib Toumi, "1.4 Million Dead Due to Arab Uprisings," *Gulf News*, August 28, 2018, https://gulfnews.com/world/gulf/bahrain/14-million-dead-due-to-arab-uprisings-1.2271986.

12. "Yemen's Houthi Rebels Launch Missiles towards Makkah and Riyadh," *The National*, May 20, 2019, www.thenational.ae/world/mena/yemen-s-houthi-rebels-launch-missiles-towards-makkah-and-riyadh-1.863838.

13. Ken Silverstein, "Israel's Natural Gas Discoveries Are Bridging Political Divides and Are Forging Economic Ties," *Forbes*, April 18, 2019, www.forbes.com/sites/kensilverstein/2019/04/18/israels-natural-gas-discoveries-are-bridging-political-divides-and-are-forging-economic-ties/.

14. "Israel Named World's 8th Largest Arms Exporter," *The Times of Israel*, March 13, 2019, www.timesofisrael.com/israel-named-worlds-8th-largest-arms-exporter/.

15. Nektaria Stamouli, "Israel, Greece and Cyprus Back EastMed Gas Pipeline," *The Wall Street Journal*, December 20, 2018, www.wsj.com/articles/israel-greece-and-cyprus-back-eastmed-gas-pipeline-11545330357.

16. Marton Dunai and Jeffrey Heller, "EU Eastern States Say Bloc Must Show More Support for Israel," *Reuters*, July 19, 2017, www.reuters.com/article/us-hungary-israel-idUSKBN1A40WZ.

17. Jonathan Lis, "Netanyahu Meets with Reelected Kenyan President, Other African Leaders," *Haaretz.com*, November 28, 2017, www.haaretz.com/israel-news/netanyahu-meets-with-reelected-kenyan-president-other-african-leaders-1.5627092.

18. Tamar Beeri, "Israel 5778 in Numbers: 25,000 New Olim, 89% of Israelis Are Happy," *The Jerusalem Post*, September 4, 2018, www.jpost.com/Israel-News/Israel-5778-in-numbers-25-thousand-new-Olim-89-percent-of-Israelis-are-happy-566475.

CHAPTER 9—WHEN THE RESTRAINER STOPS RESTRAINING

1. "Facts About the 1889 Flood," *Johnstown Area Heritage Association*, www.jaha.org/attractions/johnstown-flood-museum/flood-history/facts-about-the-1889-flood/.

2. "Who Is Pastor Apollo Quiboloy?," *Apollo Quiboloy*, April 12, 2019, www.apolloquiboloy.com/who-is-pastor-apollo-quiboloy/.

3. "Kingdom of Jesus Christ TNAEN | Pastor Apollo Quiboloy," *Kingdom of Jesus Christ*, https://kingdomofjesuschrist.org/.

BEHOLD ISRAEL

Behold Israel is a nonprofit organization founded and led by native Israeli Amir Tsarfati. Its mission is to provide reliable and accurate reporting on developments in Israel and the surrounding region.

———————

Through Behold Israel's website, free app, social media, and teachings in multiple languages, the ministry reaches communities worldwide. Amir's on-location teachings explain Israel's central role in the Bible and present the truth about current events amidst global media bias against Israel.

Learn more at **BeholdIsrael.org**

To learn more about Harvest House books and
to read sample chapters, visit our website:

www.harvesthousepublishers.com

HARVEST HOUSE PUBLISHERS
EUGENE, OREGON